Other Books by Robert DeGroot

Hard Copy Books

- Trance Formed Body
  (Paperback: Doctor Hypnosis,
  2015)
- Psychology for Successful
  Selling
  (Hardback: Branden Press,
  1988)

e-Books
Sales Training Titles

- Value Selling Strategies
  P.R.O.S.P.E.C.T. Model
- Negotiating Value
- The Hunt: Prospecting for New
  Business
- Time & Territory Management
- Goal Setting for Success
- Conditioning the Mind for
  Success
- Competitor Analysis
- Persuasive Language of Selling
- Rapid Trust & Rapport Building
- Profile and Qualify
- Key Decision-Maker Roles
- Research Prospect & Competitor
- Telephone Cold Call and Voice
  Mail Strategies
- Passive Letter Contact Series
- Interest Mailer Contact Series
- Keep In Touch Contact Series
- Networking Contact Strategy
- Asking for Referrals
- Teleblitz
- Funnel Management
- Ratio Management

- Block the Competition
- Benefit Questions Create
  Attitudes

e-Books
Sales Management Titles

- Career Path for Sales
  Professionals
- Interviewing and Hiring
- Sales Professionals Performance
  Appraisal
- Sales Coach
- Peer-to-Peer Sales Coaching
- Creating and Leading a
  Motivating Sales Culture
- Management Methods that
  Motivate
- Effective Meeting Planning and
  Facilitating
- Reseller Strategy

e-Books
Customer Service Titles

- Active Listening Skills for
  Business
- Defusing Customer Anger
- Problem Solving Model for
  Business
- Managing Customer
  Expectations
- E-mail Etiquette for Business
- Telephone Etiquette for
  Business
- Stress Control at Work

About the Author

Robert "Bob" DeGroot, MEd, DCH, is the founder and president of Sales Training International. He is an author, counselor, consultant, sales professional, and trainer with more than thirty years of experience in sales, training, and psychology.

After completing his military service in the US Coast Guard, he attended college where he earned a Bachelor's in Psychology and a Master of Education in School Psychology from Texas State University. Later in life, he earned a Doctorate in Clinical Hypnotherapy from the American Institute of Hypnotherapy. He's had rewarding careers in both the mental health sciences and in sales.

The magic in sales happened for Bob when he discovered the psychology that made sales techniques work successfully in some situations but not in others. His studies in human motivation, buying behavior, and persuasion led him to develop a different perspective that is evident in this latest book.

Bob is the author of *Psychology for Successful Selling* (Branden Books, 1988), and *Trance Formed Body* (Doctor Hypnosis, 2015). Additionally, he's written and developed more than seventy training courses, fifty web-based training courses, and forty plus e-books in the professions of psychology, sales, sales management, and customer service.

Objection Free Selling

Objection Free Selling
How to Prevent, Preempt, and Respond to Every Sales Objection You Get

Customized Editions: For information about customized editions and corporate sales, please contact Sales Training International 1-281-367-5599 Info@SalesHelp.com

Published by: Sales Training International
5781 Cape Harbour Drive STE 607
Cape Coral, Florida 33914
1-281-367-5599
www.SalesTrainingInternational.com
www.ObjectionFreeSelling.com

Objection Free Selling: How to Prevent, Preempt, and Respond to Every Sales Objection You Get

ISBN: 978-0-9864058-3-9 (Paperback)
Library of Congress Control Number: 2016910781

ISBN: 978-0-9864058-4-6 (e-book: .mobi)
ISBN: 978-0-9864058-5-3 (e-book: .ePub)

1. Objection handling, 2. Objection preventing, preempting, and responding, 3. Overcoming sales objections, 4. Selling skills

R051017

Table of Contents

Preface

The Buyer Beliefs you'll encounter in this book are based on the psychology of human motivation. In my first book, *Psychology for Successful Selling* (Branden Books, 1988), I provided the results of my research on buyer behavior to formulate a model that could consistently and reliably explain how buyers became motivated to buy. The questions used in this project involved discovering what a buyer would have to believe about a product/service before they would buy?

Test this yourself. Before you buy something, this book for example, what must you believe about it? And if you didn't believe that, what objection(s) would you have? But, if you did believe that from the beginning, what happens to the objection? It never enters your mind!

The core research demonstrated that when a specific Buyer Belief is missing or weak, an objection related to that belief is raised in the prospect's mind (just as it did for you). The obvious way to prevent objections then is to put each belief in place before the objection normally occurs in the sales process.

This is how I conceived the idea that objections could be systematically prevented by establishing the primary Buyer Beliefs with the customer before they erupted into objections.

Knowing we were on the right track, we wanted to demonstrate that because the Buyer Belief strategy is based on the principles of human psychology, it would work regardless of product or service or industry. That led us to expand the research project by building it into our training and coaching programs. Now we could automatically collect the data and compare it with the model. This would also enable us to involve thousands of salespeople across industries. The results caused me to modify the original seven belief process into a ten belief model which more accurately explained the psychology of buyer motivation.

No other book on the market today focuses on "preventing" objections as the primary strategy and that because the process is based on missing Buyer Beliefs, it can take care of all the objections you get.

"Preempting" objections is still not common because until now salespeople had no reliable way to know which objections to bring up. Who wants to bring up objections the buyer may not have thought about?

Now with our unique Competitor Analysis, salespeople can discover the objections to expect to be generated by each competitor. And yes, it provides the process to discover the information needed to neutralize them.

Even better, this Competitor Analysis helps uncover your Unique Selling Points that will create objections for the competitor.

No other book on the market will show you how to prevent, preempt, and respond to the "unanswerable" objections that you sometimes get. This one does.

Finally, this book provides examples of how to prevent, preempt, and respond to each of the 85 most common sales stopping objections. Scan the list starting on page eight and make note of those that are similar to the ones you get. Look them up in the book and personalize the recommendations to your sales situation.

Just imagine what it would have been like if your boss on your first day at work in sales had said, "Here's a 'sales strategy book' that has every objection our sales team gets for each of our products/services when selling against each of our competitors. This book has strategies and tactics you can use to PREVENT objections from entering the prospect's mind. But if you see on the Competitor Analysis that the objection already exists, then look at the examples of how to PREEMPT it and if need be, the scripted examples of how to RESPOND using tactics our team has used successfully in the past. Go ahead and personalize them to your style."

What would that book have been worth to you?

Get this book now and start customizing and personalizing the strategies and tactics for each and every objection you get. Build your own sales strategy book. How great will you feel when you can handle any objection that comes your way?

"A year from now you may wish you had started today."
Karen Lamb, Author

Get started today, buy the book now, and never again get an objection you can't handle!

Bob DeGroot

How to Use This Book

This book is divided into two parts. Part 1 contains the knowledge and skills necessary to implement all the strategies provided in Part 2. Part 2 provides multiple strategies for each of the "85 Most Common Sales Stopping Objections" organized and categorized by the missing Buyer Belief that causes them. Each Buyer Belief chapter (16 – 24) starts with the general information and strategies to establish that Buyer Belief to eliminate the objections in that category. It then continues with specific examples of how to PREVENT, PREEMPT, and RESPOND to all the objections listed in that category.

Quick Start Guide:

In Part 1:
- List the objections you get.
- Identify the missing Buyer Beliefs that cause them.
- Uncover hidden objections using the Competitor Analysis and identify your Unique Selling Points.
- Skim through the next 60 pages for a quick review of the knowledge and skills used to implement all the strategies recommended for all the objections or skip ahead to Part 2.

Go to Part 2:
- Read the chapter opening remarks and general strategies for the category of objections in which your objection falls.
- Go to the specific objections you selected and choose from optional strategies provided those that would work best for you.

Return to Part 1
- Learn any of the skills that you don't already know but need in order to implement the recommendations you selected.
- Do a complete review of all the knowledge and skills provided in the first 79 pages to find the additional hidden gems that will boost your sales.

Part 1

- List the objections you get.
- Identify the missing Buyer Beliefs that cause them.
- Uncover hidden objections using the Competitor Analysis and identify your Unique Selling Points.
- Skim through the next 60 pages for a quick overview of the knowledge and skills used to implement all the strategies recommended for all the objections or skip ahead to Part 2 to select the objection handling strategies that will work for you.

Chapter 1: Buyer Beliefs

Most sales process models will let objections slip through. You can tell this is true by noting there is a chapter or discussion in the book or a module in the training to teach you how to handle them. Some talk about "responding" to objections, while others take a more aggressive approach of "overcoming" them.

There is no mention of "preventing" or even "preempting" objections. Preventing an objection from entering the prospect's mind is very different from overcoming or responding to it once it's out there with all the negative emotional energy attached. Why wait until that happens?

To get to where you can prevent and preempt objections, as well as respond to them, you'll need to:

- Understand how objections are caused by specific missing or weak Buyer Beliefs.
- Identify the missing or weak Buyer Beliefs that are causing the objections you get.

There are three basic ways to handle objections:

1. **Prevent** them from entering the prospect's mind.
2. **Preempt** known objections when the timing is best for you.
3. **Respond** to expressed objections using a consistently effective formula.

Interestingly, the strategies used to prevent objections are easier to use than those deployed when preempting them which are easier than using the methods for responding to them.

Definitions

Objections are legitimate criticisms about your products, services, company, and self, based on what the prospect currently knows. It means that prospects can make "new favorable decisions" once they get new or redefined information that answers the "criticisms."

Unanswerable objections are those with no direct answer. The prospect objects because they want something you can't offer but your competitor can.

Conditions look like objections but they are not. Conditions are the minimum specifications or requirements that must be met for the customer to benefit from the purchase and at the same time not be harmed by the purchase. Treat conditions as objections until you confirm they are indeed required specifications.

Missing Buyer Beliefs Cause Objections

Before you buy something, what must you believe? For example, in business, you would have to believe that you have a "need." And if you don't have that belief, what objection would you give? "Don't need it" comes to mind.

What would you have to believe about price? If you didn't believe that, what objection would you give?

What else must you believe? And if you didn't what objection would you give?

Asking these questions will provide you with your own proof about how important these beliefs are to objection-free selling. Since you're the "buyer" in this example and the "beliefs" are yours, we'll refer to them as "Buyer Beliefs." There are ten basic Buyer Beliefs.

As you review each belief, put yourself in the position of the buyer and ask what objections you would give if you didn't have that belief? Conversely, recognize that the objection itself can help identify the missing or weak Buyer Belief.

Buyer Belief 1: Need Exists
A need is a gap between the current situation (problem) and a more desirable condition (solution). Related objections when the belief "need exists" is missing:
- *Not interested.*
- *Already have someone.*
- *Don't need it.*

Buyer Belief 2: Responsibility
The person has or shares the responsibility to fill the need. Related objections when the belief "responsibility" is missing:
- *I'm only getting the information for my boss.*
- *My job is to qualify suppliers.*

Buyer Belief 3: Authority
The person has or shares the authority to fill the need. Related objections when the belief "authority" is missing:
- *I need to talk with my _____ before I can make that decision.*

- *My boss won't authorize anything.*

The Buyer Beliefs "Responsibility" and "Authority" are combined going forward in this book because the preventing, preempting and responding strategies are essentially the same. They will be addressed separately when they are not the same.

Buyer Belief 4: Discomfort Felt

The needs the prospect has are strong enough to cause discomfort. Related objections when the belief "discomfort felt" is missing:

- *Just send me your literature.*
- *Don't have time to discuss it now.*
- *We'll get by with what we have now.*

Buyer Belief 5: Need has Priority

The discomfort felt is great enough so that this need has priority over other needs. Related objections when the belief "need has priority" is missing:

- *No money budgeted, call me next year.*
- *We have too many other things in front of this.*
- *We need to think this over.*

Buyer Belief 6: Type of Solution

The prospect believes your type of solution will be successful in satisfying the needs. Related objections when the belief "type of solution" is missing:

- *We've never had good results with ____.*
- *You don't have what we need.*
- *I need better quality than what you offer.*

Buyer Belief 7: Capability and Credibility

You, your product, service, and company have the capability and credibility to satisfy the need. You have the necessary levels of trust and rapport. Related objections when the belief "capability and credibility" is missing:

- *We want someone in our industry.*
- *How do you know it will do that?*
- *I've never heard of your company.*

Buyer Belief 8: Best Solution

Your solution, to the exclusion of competing solutions, will best satisfy the need. Related objections when the belief "best solution" is missing:

- *Don't see any reason to change.*
- *Why should I buy from you?*
- *I am happy with where I am buying now.*

Buyer Belief 9: Return on Investment

The price for the solution is less than the cost of the problem. Costs can be financial, subjective (hassle), or emotional (frustration). Related objections when the belief "ROI" is missing:

- *Your price is too high.*
- *I don't have the time* (subjective value).
- *Not in the budget.*

Buyer Belief 10: Plan Will Succeed

Your plan to meet the need will succeed. Related objections when the belief "plan will succeed" is missing:

- *They will never buy in to it.*
- *It's too much trouble to change.*
- *This is a lot to think about.*

Think about the last sale you lost. Can you identify which Buyer Belief(s) were weak or missing? Now, think about a sale you won. Can you identify any Buyer Beliefs that were weak or missing, regardless of whether you put them in place or not? In a business setting, what is the probability the decision-makers (team) would have bought without having all 10 beliefs?

You Only Get Objections in a Few Categories

Our classroom and field validated research indicate that most salespeople get the vast majority of objections in just three or four of the ten Buyer Belief categories. This happens because several Buyer Beliefs are put into place through other ways, ranging from the company's literature to the buyer's knowledge and experience.

Further, our research indicates that once you learn how to prevent, preempt, and respond to two or three objections in each category, you can now handle all the objections in that category.

85 Most Common Sales Stopping Objections

Following is a list of the 85 most common sales stopping objections, categorized by the Buyer Belief typically missing when the objection comes up. Check the ones you get and add them to your list so you can see the categories where you will want to focus your efforts first.

The page numbers are provided (in parenthesis) where you can find the specific strategies for each objection in Part 2.

Objection Category 1: Need Exists (81)
1. Not interested. (83)
2. Already have someone. (87)
3. We are satisfied with current supplier. (90)
4. Don't need it. (93)
5. We do it internally with our people. (95)
6. I can't use anymore _____. (97)

Objection Categories 2 & 3: Responsibility/Authority (100)
7. My boss won't authorize anything. (101)
8. It will never get through the system. (104)
9. I have to consult with _____. (107)
10. That's not my area. (108)
11. That has value but not for me. (110)
12. Home office requires we use _____. (112)
13. We have to use your competitor. (114)
14. S/he isn't here anymore. (118)

Objection Category 4: Discomfort Felt (121)
15. Just send me your literature. (123)
16. Don't have time to discuss this now. (125)
17. No one is paying attention to this area. (127)
18. We'll muddle through. (129)
19. It's too much hassle. (131)
20. We won't use it. (133)

Objection Category 5: Need has Priority (137)
21. No money budgeted, call me next year. (138)
22. We're cutting back. (140)
23. Not a priority now. (142)
24. Timing is not right; see me next month/year. (145)
25. I need to think this over. (147)
26. Too many things in front of this. (150)

Objection Category 6: Type Solution Will Work (153)
27. It just won't work for us. (154)
28. Never had good results with _____. (156)
29. This isn't for us. (159)
30. Don't want to stick our necks out on this. (161)
31. You don't have what we need. (163)
32. Your lead times are too long. (166)
33. Management is taking a different track. (168)
34. I need better quality than what you offer. (170)

Objection Category 7: Capability & Credibility (173)
35. We want someone in our industry. (175)
36. How do you know it will do that? (177)
37. Never heard of you. (180)
38. You're not large enough to handle the job. (182)
39. I don't like your company. (184)
40. I don't like your products/services. (186)
41a. You don't understand our problems. (Needs not identified) (188)
41b. You don't understand our problems. (Trust issue) (190)
41c. You don't understand our problems. (Company credibility issue (193)
42. Your track record isn't strong enough. (195)
43. Had a bad experience with your company. (197)
44. That can't be done. (199)
45. I don't believe it. (201)
46. I've never heard of your company. (203)
47. You'll have to prove that to me. (205)
48. Never had good results with _____. (207)
49. Your _____ is not good enough. (209)
50. We only buy "name brands." (211)
51. You don't have what we need. (213)

Objection Category 8: Best Solution (216)
52. Don't see any reason to change. (218)
53. We've got to look at a number of suppliers. (221)
54. Been doing business with them for years. (224)
55. Not sure yours will work as well. (226)
56. My brother-in-law is in the business. (228)
57. Don't see any difference. (230)
58. What makes you different? (232)
59. Why should I buy from you? (235)
60. We do it internally with our people. (237)
61. We want a band-aid, not a full work over. (239)
62. Costs too much to change to your products. (242)
63. We just like your competitor's product. (243)

Objection Category 9: Return on Investment (247)
64. Not in the budget. (248)
65. Your competitor does it for less. (251)
66. Your price is way out of line. (254)
67. Costs too much to change to your products. (256)
68. I can't justify spending that much money. (258)
69. My boss will never approve it (money). (259)
70. Your price is too high. (262)
71. We need a better price. (264)
72. Can't afford it. (267)
73. You'll have to do better than that. (269)
74. Sharpen your pencils. (272)

Objection Category 10: Plan Will Succeed (275)
75. No one will use it. (276)
76. Can't see how we could implement it. (278)
77. Too much risk. (280)
78. Change is tough to do around here. (282)
79. Too much trouble. (285)

80. They will never buy in to it. (287)
81. I'm not comfortable with this idea yet. (289)
82. This is a lot to think about. (291)
83. They will resist doing it. (293)
84. We need time to adjust to this. (297)
85. Don't know how to tell my supplier "no." (300)

Throughout your career as a sales professional, let me urge you to keep your own master list of objections and create your own binder of the objection handling strategies that work for you. Create "flash cards" with the objection on one side and how you'll handle it on the reverse side.

Selling is doing what's necessary to ensure each of these 10 beliefs is in place with the key decision-makers. There are a lot of different ways this can be done.

That means you don't need to learn a new sales model. The one you have now may work fine except in a few places where you're getting objections. All you need to do is plug the correct strategies into your current sales model in the right places to handle these objections.

Think about how manufacturers and service providers follow a step-by-step process to produce their products and services. When a defect occurs, they stop the process, find the error that caused it, and fix it to prevent the same defects from recurring in the future. That's not any different from what you're doing here. Consider that an objection is an error in the sales process. Now you have the means to fix it and "prevent" that objection from happening again.

Chapter 2: Competitor Analysis

The cornerstone of competitive selling is the Competitor Analysis. When going up against a specific competitor you would use the Competitor Analysis to:

- Identify the objections you'll get (spoken or not) and discover the information you need to neutralize them.
- Develop the information you need to answer the unanswerable objections.
- Identify your Unique Selling Points (USPs) and positioning strategy.
- Discover the information you can use to establish needs for the unique capabilities (USPs) the thing you sell, can bring the customer.

Select a weak competitor for your first Competitor Analysis. Draw a square and divide it into four quadrants.

Quadrant 1 (Q1): The Competitor's Perceived Strengths (upper left quadrant): The competitor based objections you get come from their perceived strengths.

Competitor Analysis

Competitor _____ Product/Service _____ Date ____

Competitor's Perceived Strengths	Your Neutralizing Capabilities
Competitor's Weaknesses	Your Strengths (USP/FAB)

What strengths or capabilities do they consistently point out in their sales presentations, website, advertisements, and literature? Why do customers buy from them?

Quadrant 2 (Q2): Your Neutralizing Capabilities (upper right quadrant): One for one, neutralize their strengths. What capability do you have that neutralizes the first strength you listed? For example, they're big, you're big; it's a wash. Move on to the next one.

If you cannot neutralize a competitor's strength by offering something the same or better, then it becomes an **"unanswerable objection."** This simply means that there is no direct equalizing capability you can offer. For example, they're big with lots of resources; you're small with very few resources. Flag it. You'll learn how to handle unanswerable objections later in the book.

Quadrant 3 (Q3): Competitor's Weaknesses (lower left quadrant): The Competitor's Weaknesses quadrant appears below their perceived strengths. Look not only to the specific product or service but also at the competitor's company itself. All companies have weaknesses. Look at their business model, capabilities, and how they do business. Dig hard and deep.

Quadrant 4 (Q4): Your Strengths (lower right quadrant): First counter each of the competitor's weaknesses with a strength you have. These are your **Unique Selling Points (USPs)** when up against this specific competitor.

Next, look for any other "strengths" you have that are not listed and list them in Quadrant 4. Then, go back into the competitor's weakness box (Q3) and record the corresponding weakness. Use the "Differentiating Commodities" list (below) to discover more USPs. Talk with others in your company about differentiators, and then search the competitor's literature and website to verify that the competitor doesn't have those identified. Later you'll learn how to use your USPs to guide your Research Questions to verify the existence of this capability supplied by the competitor or compensated for through some other means.

Differentiating Commodities

We developed the following list working with companies that sell pure commodities to help them find ways to differentiate themselves. Many of us with clearly differentiated products and services often overlook some of the less obvious game-changing capabilities. Use this list to:

- Stimulate your thinking to identify less obvious differentiating factors.
- Find the top-ten areas where you can quantifiably or qualitatively differentiate yourself.

Add items into your Competitor Analysis and then check to make sure the named competitor doesn't also have them. Don't worry if you're unsure. Coming up, you'll learn how to use Research Questions to validate all USPs.

Company: Organizational infrastructure, future plans, what you (they) emphasize such as quality, team, planning, financial stability, communications, corporate integrity, inter-departmental knowledge, reputation, experience in industry, Internet presence, e-commerce capabilities, user-friendliness, Apps, and track records such as safety and environmental.

Personnel: Training, commitment, capabilities, special skills/departments, experience in the industry, quality of staff, accessibility, and turnover that impacts relationships.

Facilities: Location, number, inventory size, redundancies backup, modernization, capabilities, and accessibility.

Materials: Feedstock quality, source/availability, procurement processes, uniform product, and quality specifications.

Manufacturing: Product line breadth and depth, product reputation, reliability engineering, lead time requirements, special or proprietary manufacturing processes or equipment, product consistency, quality assurance/controls, safety and environmental record, custom capabilities, flexibility, real-time order status monitoring, outsourcing, short notice changes, special size orders and other capabilities.

Distribution: Distribution system, packaging, shipping and transporting, tracking and monitoring, inventory, special arrangements, disposal and EPA standards, "just in time" delivery and inventory capabilities.

Research & Development: R & D capabilities, focus (customer, market, product, or service), technical support for unique customer needs.

Customer Support Services: Order center, on call 24-hours a day, customer service follow up calls, marketing research for customer, specialized product and service training to aid in troubleshooting, soft skills training, knowledgeable staff, technical support services, quick resolution of problems, automatic escalation process, documentation, warranties, guarantees, simplified paperwork, easy ordering process, customer interaction analysis.

Sales: Low customer to Representative ratio, focus on customer relationships, team approach, knowledge of customer's business, corporate account manager, national account manager, diagnostic needs analysis, consultative value-based approach to selling, "partnering" relationships, accessibility, specialists, technical competence, and responsiveness to customer needs.

After you've conducted a half-dozen or so Competitor Analyses, you'll have a list of three to five strong Unique Selling Points to use when working with prospects where the current competitor is unknown.

And to make sure you're fully prepared, you should also add to the list of objections competitors create for you in Q1, those created by universal product and service weaknesses (Type Solution) along with challenges with you industry's reputation (Capability & Credibility).

Research Questions

Your sales strategy is to orient the prospect to areas where you are strong, the competitor is weak and the prospect has needs. You can usually safely assume that if your Features (capabilities) are unique, then the prospect will not have the Advantages and Benefits provided by them. However, this may not always be the case. Use Research Questions to:

- Find unfilled needs you can fill with your USPs.

- Validate your USPs
- Verify your competitor doesn't have these capabilities.
- Determine whether the prospect has some way to compensate for not having your USPs.
- Lay the groundwork for opening the FAB / TEA value selling process discussions

Use your Unique Selling Points (USPs) to guide discussions with the various decision-makers. Take your list of USPs and categorize them where they would impact the customer the most:

1. **Prospect's products and services**: USPs related to helping make the prospect's products and services better. USPs related to how their sales strategy may be affected by your products and services.
2. **Prospect's critical processes**: USPs related to how they make their money. Map the workflow process to see the critical areas where what you sell impacts their ability to make money: increase profits, reduce costs, strengthen image, and reduce risks.
3. **Prospect's business plan**: USPs related to the prospect's strategic initiatives, goals, buying cycles, budgeting, and so on.

Your sales strategy is now clear: **focus the topics of conversation in areas where you are strong, the competitor is weak and the customer has needs!**

Chapter 3: Business, Human, & Functional Needs

Your Unique Selling Points (USPs) are used to satisfy needs your competitor cannot.

- Understand how the three categories of needs can be filled by your USPs.
- Know which specific needs in all three categories are filled by your USPs

There are three categories of needs to explore for best fit:

1. Business Needs
2. Human Needs
3. Functional Needs

Your company buys products and services that fill functional needs to meet business needs which are ultimately driven by the desire to fill fundamental human needs. The more needs (in all three categories) you can meet, the stronger your competitive position becomes.

1. Four Universal Business Needs

All businesses have four basic business needs.

- **Profit Needs**: Increase ability to generate profitable revenues.
- **Efficiency Needs:** Reduce costs of operation.
- **Security Needs:** Lessen vulnerability in their marketplace and minimize internal risk.

- **Image Needs:** Match company image to corporate and target market expectations.

2. Four Fundamental Human Needs

While each of the human needs can stand-alone as a motivator, they most often work in combination with other human needs to create another need. Human needs are the ultimate motivators.

- **Money Needs:** Able to buy the necessities of life such as food and shelter. Money can also be used to buy symbols of success when coupled with the esteem and pleasure needs.
- **Safety Needs:** Freedom from fear of loss or harm to self, possessions, and others (persons or groups) with whom we identify. They can also include the needs for health, well-being, and power.
- **Esteem Needs:** Feel confident in our ability to meet the challenges and solve the problems the world throws in front of us. Successful problem-solving abilities build and strengthen self-esteem. These also include our needs for love, affection, acceptance, confidence, and achievement.
- **Pleasure Needs:** Living our passion, doing what we value, doing what we like to do. These activities (and purchases to support them) give us pleasure. Order, symmetry, closure, happiness, and beauty are also a part of these needs.

Human needs will influence a person's buying behavior, even when a business need or a functional need is the focus. This means that you can let the prospect know that you are helping them meet these human needs by the language you use when discussing your product or service. For example, if the business security needs are driving a purchase, you could use words such as warranty, solid, reliable, durable, and others to reinforce that you will meet this need. You could also point out how you minimize any personal risk (human safety needs) the buyer might incur as a result of sticking their necks out to buy from you. Using the stepped based closing strategies in Chapter 11 is one way to do this.

3. Functional Needs

People buy things because they will fill some functional need that will, in turn, fill a business need or a human need. For example, a car jack will raise the car to change a flat tire which then meets the human need for safety. Or a remote control meets the functional need to change the channel without getting up which in turn meets the human pleasure needs. Or an insulated cup meets the functional need to keep your beverages hot or cold, which in turn, meets the pleasure need.

Companies fill their business needs by buying things that meet functional needs that in turn meet one or more of their four universal business needs. For example, purchasing self-cleaning equipment meets the efficiency need or adding a new product to sell meets the profit need. All Advantages (Feature, Advantages, and Benefits) meet a functional need and all Benefits meet one or more of the business and human needs. Sometimes the needs being filled are obvious and sometimes not. You can always make them obvious by the way in which you write them.

For example, a plastic container won't rust (functional need) which will then lower the company's risk (security need to minimize risk) when they transfer the caustic material from the rusting container to a new one. Meeting the functional need (won't rust) also meets the efficiency need to reduce costs (do away with the replacement budget), and it meets the human needs of security and pleasure (not having to clean rust stains, transfer product, put on cumbersome safety gear, and so on).

You choose which needs to use (emphasize) based on what you discover about the company and the decision-makers with whom you're interacting.

Chapter 4: Decision-Makers

In most B2B sales opportunities, six different types of decisions will be made. One person can make five of the six decision types, or there may be many people making just one type of decision. These different types of decisions are made by people in corresponding roles. You can tell which role they're in by the questions they ask. Use this list of Key Decision Maker Roles to:

- Understand the different types of decisions customers make about what you sell.
- Ensure you've identified the key decision-makers within the prospect's company.
- Identify the bias each decision-maker has toward you, your products/service and your company.
- Know the strategies used to move decision-makers to a positive bias.

Key Decision-Making Roles

To better understand these roles, think about a customer you know well and put names to the descriptions.

- **Final Authority:** Interested in Return on Investment (ROI), Return on Assets (ROA), and Rate of Return (ROR). This role is responsible for all the budgets you impact and can move money from one budget to another. This is the right level to call on for most sales opportunities.

- **Specifier:** Interested in performance specifications and cost-justification. They are usually functional area managers, but they could also be consultants hired by the company to find and sort through potential products, services, and suppliers.

- **Negotiator:** Interested in the ratio of the number of Features to the quoted price. They are usually, but not always, found in Purchasing Departments where they may buy thousands of different items on a list. Because of this sheer volume and variety, they may not know anything about what they're buying, but will often start the conversation demanding a discount.

- **End User:** Interested in user-friendliness and functionality. This includes how easy it is to do business with your company and get support when needed.

- **Coach:** They are inside the buying loop and will guide you through the buying process. "Mentors" are biased in favor of you and can become your "Champions." If they help you get the meetings, but not necessarily get involved with the decisions, they become your "Sponsors."

- **Recommenders:** These people are outside the buying loop. They could be disinterested third parties with no stake in the outcome. They could be others who have used your products and services before or who simply know you and are willing to recommend you.

Decision-Maker Bias

Decision-makers are also biased for you, neutral, or against you. Later you'll learn how we use the FAB / TEA Benefit Questions to move the person from negative to positive. You'll also learn how we use the three-step method for defusing anger and other negative emotions to move a blocker to a more positive position. Here is a brief description along with the basic strategies used to move them toward a more positive bias.

- **Champions:** Know you well and can run interference for you. They sell for you internally when you're not around. You create Champions by asking them about the benefits they, and particularly what others in the organization will get when they own your USPs.
- **Favorable:** Would prefer you, but are not broad-based enough in their understanding of the Advantages and Benefits you offer to be Champions. Ask them about the benefits they will get when they own your USPs.
- **Neutral:** Neither for you nor against you. What you've got or what your competitor offers is fine. Move them off dead-center by discussing USPs directed to the areas of their interest (job functions). Ask them about the benefits they will get when they own your USPs.
- **Unfavorable:** Would prefer someone other than you. May have had a bad experience with your products or is influenced by someone else in the organization. Move toward a more positive attitude by asking them about the benefits they will get from your USPs related to their role and their internal customer's role.
- **Blocker:** Could have had an unsettling experience with your company. Most likely is a Champion of your competitor. Defuse negative emotions (see Defusing Anger steps), and then ask about the benefits they will get from your USPs, to move them to a positive bias.

Chapter 5: Capability and Credibility

Without some level of credibility and trust, people just won't buy, no matter what the opportunity or price. Your company's credibility will help establish trust in you, and trust in you will help establish your company's credibility.

Understand the sources for:

- Eight different methods to build Capability and Credibility.
- Eight different methods to establish Trust and Rapport.

Be specific about which sources and methods you are using for each of your customers. If you're unsure about the level of trust you enjoy, then you should go back and review which specific methods you could use to enhance and strengthen corporate credibility and personal trust.

Standard Methods to Build Capability and Credibility

Capability and Credibility: Capability means you can to do what you say you can do. Credibility means believability. You do what you say you will do.

1. **Website:** Designed to appeal to your audience.
2. **Corporate capability and credibility brochures:** These are the professionally done brochures that tell about your company and its products/services.
3. **Testimonials:** Available on website and brochure making points about specific risk related areas.

4. **References:** People you can ask to provide specific information to prospects about how you solved a particular issue the prospect is concerned about.
5. **Partial client list:** Include companies that your target audience would know and respect.
6. **Referrals to key decision-makers:** Ask other customers or contacts at networking functions.
7. **Strategic Initiatives:** Connect your USPs to meeting the needs of corporate strategic initiatives.
8. **Tab and highlight:** Tab pages in your brochures and highlight key information you want the prospect to see. When the prospect opens the envelope and sees the tab sticking out of the top of your brochure, natural curiosity will get them to turn to that page. When they see a highlighted area, they will look at it. So now what happens to the often heard delay tactic, "Haven't had a chance to look at it yet." Gotcha! Note that you don't tab or highlight anything on medical or pharma literature. Check with your management in these and other industries to ensure there are no prohibitions against using this technique.

Standard Methods to Establish Trust and Rapport

Trust and Rapport: Trust means belief without proof. Rapport means to be in harmony with the other person or group in manners, behavior, attitudes, dress, speech, values, and other ways. Harmony means that we are very much alike in certain ways and the more you are like me; the more I believe I can predict how you will act in certain situations. Therefore, I can trust you to behave as I would behave in these situations.

1. **Pacing and Leading:** This enables you to become chameleon like. The more you are like me; the more I think I can trust how you would react or respond to different events. You can pace (approximate rather than mirror) language speed, tone, volume, cadence; posture, dress, and other behaviors. The easiest way to be successful with this method is to have an intense interest in the other person and care about what they say. When you do this, you will automatically pace them.

2. **Common Ground:** The more you have in common the stronger the trust will grow. The common ground can be anything from current events, schools attended, sports appreciated or played, hobbies, leisure activities, down to obvious areas such as the weather and traffic. It doesn't have to be a big thing. Any small thread of connection will do. As you learn more about the person and they learn more about you, the more common ground will be found.

3. **Personal Credentials:** These could include education, experience, a title that defines your expertise and authority (sales, engineer, marketing, manager). Outward signs of your role (executive, professional, or tradesman) including dress, appearance, and behavior speak volumes about you and your anticipated capabilities.

4. **Active Listening Skills:** If you sincerely try to understand another person's point of view first, then they become psychologically inclined to try to understand yours. Why? They know you understand them. How? Because you accurately repeated, asked clarifying questions, paraphrased the content, reflected the emotion, and summarized what they said. They

know you understand and feel obligated to return the courtesy.

5. **Research Questions:** Conduct your research in key areas such as how the company makes money, current strategic initiatives, and the impact you can have on their customers. This tells the customer you know what you're doing (see Research Questions in Chapter 2). Asking knowledgeable questions will establish trust and credibility. For example, think about a physician who only asks you one or two questions before prescribing treatment versus one who asks you many in-depth and on-target questions before prescribing treatment. Which physician do you feel understands you better and whose treatment plan would be more trustworthy and credible?

6. **FAB / TEA Formula:** Coming up you'll learn how to use the FAB / TEA formula to communicate your Advantages and Benefits through questions. This ensures the prospect makes the claims rather than someone they don't know or fully trust.

7. **Irrefutable logic:** Work toward getting agreement on the logical solution before determining who would implement it. Make sure your USPs are a part of the selection criteria.

8. **Benefits Question:** Decisions to buy are always powered by emotion, and then often backed by logic to justify them. You will learn to use the Benefit Question and the Creating Attitudes formula to bond both logic and emotion in an extraordinarily powerful justification process in which the buyer learns to trust and champion their own decisions.

Chapter 6: Features, Advantages, Benefits (FAB)

To be functionally useful in the sales process which includes identifying needs, quantifying value, and influencing specifications, your Unique Selling Points must be converted into the persuasive language of sales: Features, Advantages, and Benefits (FAB). Use the FAB format to:

- Create FABs that are irrefutably logical (IFTTT logic statements, "IF This, Then That.").
- Test your FABs to ensure they meet your targeted Functional, Business and Human Needs.
- Prepare FABs to be used in the FAB / TEA formula, you'll learn soon about, to establish seven of the ten Buyer Beliefs.

Your Features provide the Advantages and Benefits (FAB). The Advantages explain the Feature and tell why it's a better way to deliver Benefits. The Benefits point to what the customer gets to meet their business and human needs.

Each FAB, which when read in any order (BAF, ABF, AFB, and so on), will show an **irrefutable logic**. For example, "To reduce the replacements you buy (B) caused by rust, you'll need use containers made from a material such as plastic (F) that won't rust (A)."

Features (F): Characteristic
Advantages (A): Explain the Feature and fill functional needs
Benefits (B): Fill business and human needs that motivate people to buy

Feature (F): Made of Plastic.

Advantage (A): Won't rust. That meets the functional need to stop the rust (competitor's containers are metal and have to be continually replaced due to rust).

Benefit (B): Don't need to budget money to replace containers due to rust. This meets business needs of lowering and eventually eliminating this particular budgeted item.

Features, Advantages, and Benefits provide structure for the persuasive language of selling. Note that one Feature can have more than one Advantage and more than one Benefit. And it could take several Features bundled together to provide a high-powered set of Advantages and Benefits.

The FAB structure works by writing them so they are irrefutably logical ("if this, then that"). Plastic (F) won't rust (A) which means rusting container replacement budget can go away (B).

You can use the FAB structure to look for the signs and symptoms that suggest the prospect doesn't have your USP's Feature. For example, what would you ask or look for that would indicate they don't have your USP's Feature? With our container example, you might see rust stains, disgruntled employees who have to move product from one rusting container to another that's not rusted, rusted container replacement budget, and so on. These are the missing Advantages and Benefits provided by the Feature. By finding the signs or symptoms of the missing Advantages and Benefits of the USP's Feature, this FAB has been validated. You've also verified your competitor is not providing this USP and you've determined that the prospect is not using some other method to compensate.

Your Unique Selling Points (USPs) gain significant functionality in selling when they are converted to Features, Advantages, and Benefits. Not only does that tell you where to explore using your Research Questions (missing Advantages and Benefits), it is absolutely necessary to use the FAB / TEA formula for selling value.

Chapter 7: FAB / TEA Formula

The FAB / TEA formula has two parts. The first part educates the prospective customer about your Unique Selling Point's Feature (capability) and how it will meet their functional needs, and the second part guides them to identify and tell you about the Benefits they want that you can provide that will meet their business and human needs. Use this formula to:

- Educate the prospect about your USPs.
- Get the decision-makers to tell you about the how the Advantages and Benefits your USPs provide will meet their Functional, Business, and Human needs.
- Quantify what it costs the prospect not to have the Advantages and Benefits delivered by your USPs Features using their facts and figures.
- Discover the subjective and emotional values of your USPs
- Set your USP FABs as part of the specifications the prospect will use to select a supplier.
- Use the Benefit Questions to rehearse the prospect to sell internally for you when you're not around and to create favorable attitudes toward you.

All "value selling" models use a strategically designed interview to establish the value of the solution to minimize price pressure. The FAB / TEA formula does that and much more. This model can establish seven of the ten Buyer Beliefs including:

- Need Exists

- Discomfort Felt
- Need has Priority
- Type of Solution will Work
- Capability & Credibility
- Best Solution
- Return on Investment

These beliefs are listed in the sequence in which they normally occur. Often, by focusing your efforts on establishing a belief that comes later in the sequence will by default, establish the earlier related beliefs.

FAB / TEA Two Part Process

The first part of the formula uses your Features and Advantages to educate the prospect and the second part asks strategic questions about the specific Benefits delivered by the Feature.

F. Feature
A. Advantage
B. Benefit

T. Tell the Feature
E. Explain it with the Advantage.
A. Ask about the Benefit.

Part 1: Educate the customer.
Tell the Feature.
Explain it with the Advantage.

Part 2: Sell with questions.
Ask about the Benefit.

For example, suppose you sell containers made of plastic for $25 each that last 100 years. You learned during your USP guided Research Questions that your competitor in this opportunity sells the same containers made of steel for $10 that after 5 years must be replaced due to rust. How would you get the customer to realize the value of your containers without telling them?

Start with the USP FAB.

Feature: Plastic.
Advantage: Won't rust.
Benefit: Lowers maintenance and replacement costs.

Next, apply the FAB / TEA formula.

Part 1. Educate: **Tell** the Feature and **Explain** it (Advantage): "The product is plastic (F) so it won't rust (A)."

Note that the Advantage explains the Feature and tells how it meets the functional need of stopping rust.

Part 2. Sell: **Ask** about the Benefits.

Target your Benefits toward both the business and human needs in the sequence that favors your product/service.

Business Needs: efficiency, profit, security, and image
Human Needs: money, safety, esteem, and pleasure

Business Need: Efficiency

- "How many containers do you need to replace each year due to rust?"
- "What about the labor costs of removing the rust stains?"
- "How much is budgeted now?"
- "Let's do the math to see how much will be left in the budget for each barrel you replace. Next, we should calculate the savings once all the containers have been replaced over the next five years."

Business Need: Security (Risk)

- "What costs are associated with transferring your product from one container to another?"
- "How much difficult is that?"
- "Are there risks involved during the transfer?"
- "What about the risks to employees doing this work?" (Human Need: Safety)
- "This is not a job they look forward to, is it?" (Human Need: Pleasure)
- "Who does this job, senior or junior people?" (Human Need: Esteem)

Business Need: Image

- "How do your customers handle it when they do a plant visit and see all these rusting containers?"
- "What does that do for your image?"

Business Need: Profit

- "Are there more profits to be had if customers aren't put off by the rusting containers?"
- "Would the direct bottom-line impact transfer to bigger dividends?"
- "Why would reducing the number of containers that rust be important for this budgeting cycle?"

You can also ask about how other decision-makers might benefit as well. For example, "Why would your VP want to push this through now?" Or you could ask, "Who else would benefit from starting the changeover now?"

Standards of Legitimacy

In many sales situations, you will find yourself interviewing people who are unaware of the actual costs associated with doing certain tasks. As such, you will need to be prepared with the "standards of legitimacy" for these costs or risk having the sale stall while the prospect looks up the numbers. Use this strategy to:

- Prevent the sale from stalling because important numbers are not readily available.
- Agree on the standards that will be used later during negotiations.
- Set up sample cost charts to use for comparison with competitors where the numbers are not known.

Standards of legitimacy are norms or industry standards. They are "rules of thumb" or guidelines used to establish the cost of certain key areas your product or service impacts. For example, if your product/service saves time, it is important to know whose time it saves, how much time it saves and how much is that time worth.

In our plastic container example, if the prospect uses four hours each week transferring product from one container to another and to clean the rust, then these "use costs" should be added to the metal containers to determine their true bottom-line costs.

What happens if the prospect does not know how much that level employee earns per hour? To maintain your momentum and keep the sale moving forward, you will need to provide a temporary guideline or standard to calculate costs.

You can determine employee costs from industry magazines, the newspaper "Help Wanted Ad's," personnel staff and so on, what the "average" technician (manager, clerk, and so on) earns hourly. Next, you add the burden rate which includes such things as matching Social Security, taxes, other overhead, and benefits.

Let's say that the employees transferring the materials from the metal containers and cleaning the rust stains earn $15.00 per hour, and the benefits package and overhead average 50% of salary. Therefore, 1.5 X $15.00 = $22.50 per hour.

Now to set the Standard you would say to the prospect, "Employees doing this type work at other companies in the area earn around $15 per hour plus a 50% benefits package bringing the burdened cost to the company of $22.50 per hour. Does that sound about right or is yours a little higher or lower? Whatever the prospect says just use it in the calculations. The exact numbers can get determined later. Your objective is at this point is to keep the sales process moving and not stalling out over the numbers.

For example, 4 hours per week X 52 weeks = 208 hours per year X $22.50 = $4,680. This is a "use cost" that must now be added to the price of the metal containers to get the total bottom-line impact for the competitor's product. Using a Balance Sheet Closing Strategy will make it very clear to the prospect the inclusive costs associated with their current supplier.

Learn about the standards associated with what you sell. For negotiations, recognize that the existence of one standard does not preclude the existence of a different and equally valid standard. For win-win outcomes, you negotiate the standards that produce the numbers rather than the numbers themselves.

Benefit Questions

You should recognize by now that a critical part of this value selling model is to ask the prospective customer questions related to the specific Benefits provided by your USP's Features and Advantages. You would use the Benefit Questions to:

- Identify quantitative, qualitative, and personal value.
- Shift the burden of proof from you to them.
- Discover others who will benefit.
- Competitor-proof your customers.
- Create positive attitudes.

1. **Quantitative Value:** When you ask quantifying questions (put a number into a calculator) you establish the value that

can help offset higher prices and prevent the price objections. For example, "How often does it happen?" "What costs are involved when it happens (people, product, time, and so on)?"

2. **Qualitative Value:** When you ask qualitative questions that provide subjective and emotional responses, you get values that motivate people to put up with the hassle of changing to your products. For example, "How difficult is the procedure?" "Does that take a lot of strength to do it?" "Do they like it?" "How do people feel when that happens?" "How frustrating is that?" It's the subjective hassle factor and the associated emotions that motivate people to take action.

3. **Personal Value:** Prospect learns the value this decision could have for them. For example, they might get a share of the savings of the improved production, they might get a promotion or a raise, or they get an award for helping the company achieve a strategic initiative. Some personal reasons they may not want to share with you and some they might not even be aware of themselves. But, recognize at the subconscious level, this thinking is going on and it's increasing their motivation to buy. This part of the process works provided you minimize the risks involved by using irrefutable logic first and references second.

4. **Shift Burden of Proof from You to Them:** The person making the claims is the person who has to offer proof to support those claims. By asking questions about the benefits, you are shifting the burden of proof from your shoulders to the prospects because they are the person making the claims, not you. And that's how you zap skepticism. When you couple this strategy with the value questions discussed above, you also move the time urgency from you to them.

5. **Discover Others Who Benefit:** You can guide them to identify the Advantages and Benefits others in the organization might get. When you expand the range of people benefiting you discover not only what's important to this decision-maker but to others as well. You are rehearsing them to sell internally for you when you're not around. And they can sell to decision-makers you can't get in to meet. They can become your Champions. For example, "How will people in your Accounting Department benefit?" "Who in particular would benefit?" "I know with our other customers, the VP of Finance is happy about the rate of return, how do you think that rate will be received by your VP of Finance." "What's the best part of this for the technicians?" "Who else would benefit from this choice?" "What would they get?" "How do we let them know?" Make the prospect feel good about helping others in their company.

6. **Create Attitudes to Competitor Proof Your Customers:** Because the process to do this is deceptively simple and the results extremely powerful, I've set it apart from the brief write-ups in this list and placed it in a section of its own called "Creating Attitudes." By doing this, I can provide a more detailed explanation of the process and I can make it stand out in the Table of Contents so you can readily find it again and again.

Chapter 8: Creating Attitudes

Beliefs are changeable. When a person learns new information that proves something different from the belief held, then the belief gets changed to align with the new information. Attitudes, however, are resistant to change regardless of the volume of information contrary to the belief. Ever wonder how teenagers, colleagues or employees get some of their attitudes?

Creating attitudes is a fairly easy process, sometimes too easy. But, if you're not paying attention to what you're doing, it can also backfire. With this in mind, I modified the procedure to make it user-friendly. I also developed a three-step process to organize its use so it can work consistently and smoothly in sales. Use this process to:

- Create favorable change resistant attitudes toward your product/service, company, and self.
- Help decision-makers defend their decisions to select you to others using irrefutable logic powered with emotional commitment and strength.
- Rehearse the decision-makers you can talk with to sell to others you cannot get in to see.
- Run interference for you.

To create favorable attitudes, ask challenging questions about each USP you've put through the FAB / TEA formula. When you challenge a belief or behavior and it is successfully defended in the mind (logic) and heart (emotion) of the defender, you've created an attitude that is resistant to change, regardless of how much credible contrary evidence you present.

The attitude is created the moment an emotion is attached to their explanation of "why" they want something. Using the question "why" in a subtly challenging manner always evokes the defense emotions. You can ask the question "why" many different ways. Often it's your tone of voice, body language, or other mannerisms that make it a challenge. The challenging question evokes the defense emotion and attaches it to the belief or behavior. That combination automatically creates an attitude.

Belief or Behavior plus Emotion equals Attitude (B+E=A). Therefore, only ask challenge style questions about things you can provide or desirable behaviors you want to see repeated more frequently with greater intensity; never about things you cannot provide or about undesirable behaviors. That means don't ask your prospect what they like about the current supplier. Your Competitor Analysis supplied you with that information.

Use this three-step process to create attitudes favorable to you:

1. Support what they say.
2. Challenge it gently and make sure they successfully defend it.
3. Support them again.

For example:

You (orient to belief to reinforce): "I like this Feature because it ___ and ___, what about you?"

Customer: "Yeah, that is nice.

You (support/challenge): It does. "Besides that, why else do you like it?"

Customer: "It has a good ____."

You (challenge): "What about your boss, how do you see her liking this?"

Customer: "Oh she'll like ____ about it."

You (support): "I totally agree with you on that."

With this simplified example, you can see how easy it is to get the prospective customer to defend not only what they like, but also how someone else in the buying loop might like it as well. When they do this, it strengthens their ability to accurately sell for you when you're not around. The stronger the defense and the more emotional the defense, the stronger the attitude becomes. Sometimes it takes two or three challenges to get the attitude locked in, which is why I like grouping two or three challenges together. For example, "Help me understand why that would be important in your company?" "How would that be received by your accounting department?" "Why would they go for it?" "What's in it for them?"

The formula is Belief plus Emotion equals Attitude (B+E=A) and the process to use it is to support, then challenge, then support. The hard fast rules are to:

- Challenge only what you can provide and never challenge what you cannot.
- Challenge only what you want and never challenge beliefs or behaviors that you do not want.

If the prospective customer asks if you offer something the competitor does, but you don't, and if you were to ask the customer "why" they wanted it, they would start explaining and defending what they want. This would clearly be to your competitor's advantage and to your detriment. Learn to say "no" in a way that will minimize any defensive emotional reaction.

Saying "No" Creates Loss

When you tell someone "no" it signals the loss of something they have or want. That evokes the grief process which includes the emotions of "anger" and "sadness." Aren't these the emotions expressed in the tantrums kids throw when they're told "no?" These emotions are a natural part of the grief process. In this section you can learn how to:

- Prevent the grief process from generating the feelings anger and sadness toward you.
- Use "erasers" to diminish the strength of negative reactions when you have to tell someone "no."
- Get the prospect on your side, even though you can't provide what they want.

Loss, real or imagined, triggers the grief process which includes the emotions of "anger" and "sadness." Yet, there are times when you do have to tell the customer you can't do or offer something. What then?

Whenever you tell the prospect you "can't do or provide" something, ALWAYS follow up immediately with something you CAN DO" separated by an eraser (but or however). For example, "I'm sorry that's not something we have, and I know that's disappointing to you. BUT, what we do offer is _____ with ___, ___, and ___ (USPs). Let's go over some advantages of this approach, and then we can see how we can make this will work for you. Fair enough?"

"But" and "however" are erasers. Meaning their job is to erase everything that was said in front of them. For example, "You've done a great job, but . . ." Notice how the first part of that sentence disappeared. "However" is also an eraser with a softer touch. It's really a matter of what you want to accomplish. Which sounds better to you?

You now know that you can minimize the sense of loss that generates anger and sadness by counterbalancing what you can't do with what you can do. Keep in mind that you'll need to provide a "gain" of three to five times more (financially, subjectively, and emotionally), than what they gave up, to completely cancel the feeling of loss. By using your Active Listening Skills and the Defusing Anger technique, you can transition them from someone who could block you, to someone who will speak favorably of you, regardless of the final outcome regarding the loss.

Chapter 9: Active Listening and Defusing Anger

The Active Listening Skills are an essential part of all sales interactions and they are an integral component for Defusing Anger. So let's take a moment now to review them both.

Everybody knows the Active Listening Skills and yet few people use them. Use these listening skills to:

- Establish a Psychological Truth: *"If you sincerely try to understand another person's point of view first (not necessarily agree with it), then they become psychologically obligated to try to understand yours."*
- Cause the prospect to elaborate on an ill-conceived objection.
- Help the prospect talk themselves out of objections.

Six Active Listening Skills

1. Provide **Acceptance Responses:** These are brief utterances that let the speaker know you're listening without interrupting their flow of thought. For example, "Okay," "Yes," "I see," "Uh-huh," or simply moving your head up and down.
2. **Repeat:** Say a keyword, phrase, or number exactly the way they said it, much like you'd do if you wanted to make sure you got the time right for a meeting or wrote a phone number correctly.
3. **Paraphrase content**. Say it using your own words.
4. **Reflect emotion**. Name the emotion. Pay attention to the emotional subtext of the conversation. This can

dramatically deepen trust and rapport if you do and the opposite if you don't.

5. **Ask Clarifying Questions:** Move from generalizations to specifics, but never challenge with the question, "why?" See the previous chapter about Creating Attitudes.

6. **Summarize:** Use repeating, paraphrasing, and reflecting in summary form to include two or more topics or steps.

When using these skills, recognize that these are "mirrored contributions." That means **you are not adding new information** unless it is to clarify what you thought you heard through an analogy, metaphor, or related example. For example, if the prospect says, "I don't like these products," you get the prospect talking so you can figure out where to go next by asking a clarifying question such as, "Don't like them?" or simply repeat, "Don't like them." But never ask, "Why don't you like them?"

It's also important to know when not to use these skills. For example, if the prospect is expressing clearly stated questions or concerns and it's obvious to the prospect that you heard and understood what they said, you can usually start with a transition sentence. For example, if the prospect were to ask, "Are these more expensive than those?" If that made sense to you, then you would NOT say, "Let me see if I understand, you want to know whether these are more expensive than those?" But, if anything is unclear, or is the least bit complex, or has an obvious emotion attached, or requires a thoughtful answer, then it would be time to use these skills.

The outcome you want is for the prospect to know you truly understand what they're saying, including the emotional energy behind it. This is how you earn the right to be heard.

Three Steps to Defuse Anger

A most useful set of skills for anyone who has to deal with all the challenges associated with delivering a product or service and sometimes falling short of the customer's expectations. Use these skills to:

- Defuse negative emotions directed toward you, your products/services, or your company.
- Pull the plug on strong negative feelings commonly tied to objections.
- Help the prospect move from a Blocker to a less destructive bias.
- Get the prospect to appreciate you, even if you were unable to solve the problem in their favor.

When you recognize any negative emotion from any person you're talking with, directed at you or not, use these steps to defuse the emotion, because ignoring emotions only serve to intensify them.

1. **Recognize:** Get it out in the open. Call it by name. This defuses the anger. Reflecting the emotion releases its power. For example, "No wonder you're upset. If that happened to me, I'd be mad too." Take care not to underestimate the intensity of the emotion. Err on the side of greater intensity. Ignoring the emotion will intensify it.

2. **Apologize:** Show you care. Offer a generic "no-fault" apology. This releases the sadness emotion that follows the release of a negative emotion. For example, "I'm really sorry that happened to you." Or, "Ouch, that's just not right!"

3. **Solutionize:** Problem-solving to prevent further loss and help them move on to objectivity and even acceptance. For example, "Let's go over this so I can talk to the right people in our organization to let them know what happened so we can keep this from happening again." Or, "That didn't work out as planned, so if you'd like, let's look at how we've helped customers compensate for this."

It may be necessary to repeat this process more than once or twice to clear or significantly reduce the intensity of all or most emotions. Making appropriate body language gestures and vocalizations can help convey your message of understanding. You don't need to agree with them, you just need to empathize.

Be sure to always err on the side of greater severity. For example, how would you feel if you were upset and someone said, "Oh, it's not that bad." Would that calm you or upset you even more? How would that make you feel about the person who said that? Now you know what to do when you encounter an upset person.

Chapter 10: Customer Value Proposition (CVP)

The Customer Value Proposition (CVP) is focused on communicating the value you bring to the customer rather than on your product/service. Use the CVP to:

- Enhance trust and earn the right to be heard by providing your understanding of the prospect's situation related to the challenges under discussion.
- Disclose the financial, subjective, and emotional costs of the problems to establish the value of the solution and bring perspective to the price you charge.
- Use the formula: product price (top line) + operational use costs + hidden costs = bottom-line to establish financial value.
- List and discuss the subjective and emotional costs and how you change those with the value you offer.
- List the steps in the plan that will guide the prospect through purchasing, implementing, and using your product/service.

The CVP consists of:

1. **Situational Analysis:** Present your understanding of the situation. This is the sum of your knowledge about the company that is relevant to the challenge under discussion. When you communicate this deep understanding about the company you establish trust and you earn the right to speak and be heard.
2. **Value:** Quantify the seriousness of the problems using the "bottom-line" formula. The "bottom-line" formula

is the sum of the price to get the product or service ("top line" number in the equation), the cost associated with using the product/service, plus any hidden costs associated with the company you choose to do business with. When you add these together you get the "bottom-line."

Price (topline)
+ Cost to use
+ Hidden Cost
= Bottom-Line

The most effective CVPs are created when using the customer's facts and figures and include financial, subjective (hassle factors), and emotional (frustrations) costs. They also cast the ongoing operating use costs and any hidden costs into the future for the useful life of the product, or term of the service agreement to show an even wider spread. If you are unable to get the numbers you need, then turn to your "standards of legitimacy" for guidance.

3. **Selection Criteria:** List the criteria to select a solution and solution provider. These would include the prospect's specifications and the USPs you set as criteria during your sales interviews using the FAB / TEA formula. Discuss how you can meet each one. Be sure to include how you will handle the subjective and emotional value issues.

For luxury and ultra-high quality items, list the components of the image you want to create in the various settings you discuss in the situational analysis. Talk about how you can do that in a way the competitor cannot (without mentioning the competitor by name).

4. **Investment:** This can be presented in a Balance Sheet Closing Strategy format, a Multi-Bid Summary Form, or in a standard table with explanations for each of the costs. Separate by the financial investment due you and the use costs the prospect will incur during implementation and ongoing operations.

5. **Plan for Implementation:** List the steps that need to be completed for the prospect to own and use your product/service. A combination of the Plan of Action Close and the Operating Plan Close (see Chapter 11) tends to work well for most sales, particularly when customized for the prospect.

Luxury and Ultra-High Quality Items and the CVP: If you sell luxury items or higher-quality items where the price or direct cost comparisons are not applicable, you can use the situational analysis to create (confirm) the image of what the prospect currently has, to the image of what they want. This is an easy way to create the gap (need).

Chapter 11: Specialized Closing Strategies

There are three categories of closing strategies that are essential to all sales processes involving products/services that are presented as solutions to problems or presented as a better way. These include the:

1. Balance Sheet Closing Strategy
2. Multi-Bid Summary Form Closing Strategy
3. Step-Based Closing Strategies

Balance Sheet Closing Strategy

So often we get involved with price objections with a prospect who doesn't understand the CVP formula to calculate the total bottom-line impact of what they buy. Instead, they simply compare the product prices (top line). Use the Balance Sheet Closing Strategy to:

- Show a side-by-side comparison of the "total cost of ownership."
- Cast the ongoing operating use costs and any hidden costs into the future for the useful life of the product or term of the service agreement to show an even wider spread.
- Prevent most objections related to "price."

To set up the Balance Sheet, create a form with three columns:

1. Column one lists the specified items such as product/service, delivery, annual maintenance items,

annualized usage items, terms, use costs, hidden costs, and so on. Include your unique selling points that you set as criteria or requirements during your sales interviews.

2. Column two has your product name in the header row.
3. Column three has your competitor's product name in the heading row.
4. Across from each item, and under the appropriate product, start listing the price to get the products, and then continue down to add the usage and hidden costs for each item you listed in column one. You will have many zeros in your column and your competitor will have hidden and use costs. If you don't know your competitor's prices, or weren't able to quantify certain costs, then simply include the dollar sign and short line to indicate to the prospect that they should fill in the information themselves. Or you can use any agreed upon standards of legitimacy. If you do, be sure to note it so that it's not confused with a number specific to this company.

Once you sum the totals, your product's bottom-line total cost of ownership will be less than your competitors. You can also cast these figures into the future. For example, if you have a three-year service agreement you can run the numbers three years into the future to show an even greater spread of costs.

A fun way to practice this closing strategy is to set your competitor's product/service price at zero then use standards of legitimacy in all the other areas. Once you total the columns, you'll know how much the competitor will have to adjust their price to get even with yours. Next, cast these numbers out for the life of the product or term of the service agreement to see an even bigger difference.

But also understand that with some products/services such as luxury items, ultra high quality, and prestige brands, you may want the price significantly higher than the competitors, with the image as the only defining difference. Again, this would come down to knowing the profile of your target market prospects matched with what you sell.

You can also add an optional Column 4 would be left blank for the prospect to fill in with another competitor if you know there is one involved.

Multi-Bid Summary Form Closing Strategy

Use a Multi-Bid Summary Form in your proposal to:

- Prevent being underbid or being outmaneuvered by your competitor.
- Submit multiple bids on one form.
- Allow the prospect to select from the options you've provided to create a customized bid package.

To set up the Multi-Bid Summary Form make a spreadsheet with five columns:

1. Column one is a listing of the items and specifications included in the proposal including the USPs you set as specifications or criteria.
2. Column two is for listing and pricing what you'd provide that minimally meets specifications.
3. Column three contains your recommendations and pricing based on your knowledge of the client's needs.

4. Column four contains what the client could get if they wanted to go the extra step for whatever reason (safety, ego, thoroughness, luxury). Include the associated pricing.

5. Column five is left blank except for a dollar sign and a line. This is where the customer would fill-in the price of the option they select (minimum, recommended or extra step).

Total the costs for each column.

There may be times when you don't want to provide something in the minimum specifications column because you don't think it will work for the customer but you know your competitor will so they can give a lower price.

If so, briefly describe what would meet the minimal requirements, and then tell why you won't provide it next to the description you provided. Now include what you would recommend and the pricing in that same column. Even though you're going to provide it again in the next "recommended" column, they need to get a total from each column.

Also, note that while the "extra step" column usually carries a higher per item price, this is not always the case. Sometimes because an item is so popular, its production cost is much lower than the other two columns (minimal specifications and recommended). In this case, you might use this same item in the first column. Be sure to footnote that's the reason for listing it there.

By using the Multi-Bid Summary format, customers often catch on to the tricks some competitors use just to get the business and then start adding the change orders.

You can also add another heading row that defines items you think would enhance the purchase laid out using the same structure as the first section. Here is where you can also list USPs you talked about but were not set as a part of the criteria and specifications package. Customers appreciate this extra effort because they may have some anxiety about missing something important when they buy. The Multi-Bid Summary Form is an extraordinarily powerful format.

If this is part of an RFI (request for information) or RFP (request for proposal), then you can use this form in the main part of your response. However, if this is part of an RFQ (request for quote) then you can only use the Multi-Bid Summary Form as part of the support package of information rather than the main body.

When there are many unknown factors that could influence the pricing one way or the other, using the Multi-Bid Summary Form makes quoting easier. We've had clients ranging from computer manufacturers to engineering firms tell us about sales they've won using this form. One client told us that one of their repeat government customers waits until they get their Multi-Bid Summary Form so they can use it to compare other bids.

Step-Based Closing Strategies

There are several Step-Based Closing Strategies to select from. They are always a part of establishing the tenth Buyer Belief (Plan Will Succeed). And they are often in play throughout the sales process. You would use these to:

- Lower the anxieties of decision-makers not familiar with buying from you (Master Plan).

- Pre-close on actions you want the prospect to take (Agenda).
- Block competitors between sales calls (Action Item Plan).
- Include a personality-guided plan that works well at the end of the CVP (Plan of Action).
- Create a coordination plan when you have several teams working on parallel tasks (Triggering Events)
- Continue to find new opportunities for repeat and new business with a customer (Operating Plan)

When prospects aren't sure what will happen next, they may understandably become anxious or fearful and get "cold feet." Also, recognize that the less the buyer knows about buying your type of solution, or the less familiar they are with how your company does business, the more detailed the steps will need to be, and the more assurances you will need to provide. You'll want to continually build and strengthen trust and rapport, as well as capability and credibility to ease the buyer's anxieties as you guide them through the buying process.

The most important way to minimize the prospect's anxieties about the workability of your proposal is to develop a very detailed plan for implementation. Take a look at six "stepped" closing strategies that work exceptionally well in these situations.

1. **Master Plan for Implementation Close:** Make a list of all the steps involved in buying from you. Getting the purchase order then becomes just another step in the process. Continue to add to this list any sub-steps that could be options for different situations. Identify the phases and milestones into which these steps fit. Add "how" each step is usually done, and then add optional

ways it can be done (Plan B). You can continually add and revise this master plan as you learn more about implementation challenges from your various customers.

2. **Agenda Close:** This closing strategy allows you to pre-close by getting the prospect to agree to the action items on the agenda at the beginning of each meeting or at the end of the meeting for the next meeting. When they agree to the agenda, they are in effect, agreeing to move forward. When the prospect says, "Okay, let's get started," you have just pre-closed on several steps in your sales process. For example: "First, I would like to give you a brief overview of our company to help orient and define some of our capabilities. Then, if I could get some information about your organization, I can quickly determine where we can help. We'll specifically want to explore (state areas of your Unique Selling Points as they relate to the four business needs). After that, if the needs are there and the cost-benefit analysis shows there's a worthwhile impact to be made, we can then start a plan to move forward. How does that agenda sound so far?"

3. **Action Items Plan Close:** This strategy identifies the actions to be taken between meetings by both buyer and seller. This is a rolling or continuous plan that documents what's been done and what needs to be done. Similar to the minutes of a meeting, but bulleted rather than lengthy text. For most people involved in a formal quality process, i.e., ISO, all meetings with actionable items require each item to be documented with the people responsible for doing each item identified. Follow-up dates must be scheduled (at least tentatively), and the people who need to be there should listed, notified and confirmed. You want to be the

person who will send an e-mail with this information. Setting the meeting may best be handled by the prospective client once they've confirmed the people they need in the meeting can attend. You'll want to confirm any people from your team who should attend as well. The psychology that makes this work is that once the prospect gets invested in carrying out this plan, with all that they have to do on their plates, they are less likely to want to engage with your competition to repeat this process and get even more action items. Remember, the quality process mandates the documentation and follow-up process. If you've ever been in a meeting where the decision-makers did not want to discuss action items, this may indeed be the reason because once they do and agree to any of them, they have to document it and follow up on the items.

4. **Plan of Action:** The Plan of Action Close includes several steps in which the first one or two have already been completed, several steps to provide feedback to the buyer, and it will include a few steps that can occur without the buyer's input. This sets up a flow that plays into a personality style that half the decision-makers you encounter have. This group has difficulty making a decision to "start" the process, so you only put them in the position of having to make a decision to "stop" the flow, which goes against their personality. Their preference is to go with the flow, keep their options open, and get lots of information (feedback). This closing strategy also supports people with the opposite personality trait. They prefer to live in a planned, structured, and organized manner. This plan works exceptionally well at the end of the Customer Value Proposition. It can also be structured using the

Triggering Events domino effect and it can be merged with the Operating Plan Close imagery strategy.

5. **Triggering Events Close:** Create a plan of action that has a domino effect of one step "Triggering" the next and so on through closure, follow-up, and new or repeat business.

6. **Operating Plan Close:** Now that they own your product/service what do they do with it to maximize the Benefits they can get. Write a list of steps they are to take when using your product/service to get the maximum benefits from it. Use words that create sensory experiences. This closing strategy works best when the person can see it, touch it, feel it, smell it, taste it, and sense emotions connected with it. Help them imagine the process of getting and using your product or service to the fullest extent without having it in front of them. This works because when they do get it in front of them; their dreams of what it would be like are now reinforced by what it actually is like.

Chapter 12: Change Management Process

There is no doubt when you ask someone to buy from you for the first time, especially if you're taking business away from a familiar competitor, you are asking them to make a change. Unless you include a change management process as a routine part of your sales process, you could accidentally elicit fear-based objections that can stop your sale. You would use this change management process to:

- Prevent fear-based reactions to change.
- Help the prospect accept and support change.

Change is difficult for most people. Psychological and biological based anxieties and fears of change can cause them to put up a huge amount of resistance. It doesn't have to be a big change that causes this reaction. Anything that moves the person from the known to the unknown will automatically elicit hypervigilance and potential fear-based objections.

But with some understanding of how and why this occurs, you'll be able to manage the change without all the negative side effects. The strategy is to build the basics of change management into your sales process.

People have two brain structures called the "Amygdalae." Among other things, one of their primary functions, particularly the one in the right hemisphere of the brain, is to help us survive by alerting us and automatically reacting to danger. These structures continually monitor our internal and external environment for anything that might provide a threat or pleasure (left hemisphere amygdala) to us. If the amygdalae sense any change in their environment, they become hyper-vigilant and ready to react (positive or negative).

Sensory input to the amygdalae bypasses the brain's normal thought and judgment structures and processes used to generate a reasoned response. This happens later, but by then the reaction has already taken place. Sensory input goes straight to the amygdalae that scan it for any vaguely related memories. If it finds one (danger or pleasure), it takes immediate nonthinking action. Its reaction is similar to automatically slamming on the brakes of your car when you sense danger on the road ahead. Or that immediate joyful reaction you feel when you hear about winning a contest. No thinking was involved, just reacting to the subconscious stimulus.

Most of us, however, have lives filled with unmanaged negative stress and are more on the alert for danger than to pleasure. For many, most change (large or small, positive or negative, past, present, or future) is regarded as a threat and the immediate nonthinking reaction is to resist. Often, this is all happening at the subconscious level and people are not even aware that they're resisting. Sometimes the prospect might just get a "gut" feeling that results in a quickly verbalized objection, and then turning away, not wanting to discuss it anymore. But now you know that resisting change is biologically based, natural, and often rooted deep within the subconscious mind.

The good news is that the amygdalae are constantly learning. That means you can train them not to cause a fear reaction to the change that could result from what you sell. In fact, with a little finesse, you can get these structures to learn to view your product and its implementation as more desirable than staying with the status quo. Make the current way the pain-inducing costly enemy and the new way, the safe and pleasurable way.

Resistance to change increases dramatically when the people involved are excluded from the process. Deciding everything for someone else is damaging to their self-esteem. People must be allowed to participate in the process or their moral will suffer, their work output will be diminished, and the many forms their pushback can take will be amazing.

That's why the people who must make the change must be fully engaged in the change process. Let them decide where they have the expertise and experience and where they lack expertise, let them make recommendations about the end result that would be helpful to them. Keep in mind that people generally don't resist something they helped create. The more they are involved, the less they will resist.

Include those affected in the process as early on as possible. They may not have control over the outcomes, but they may have control over how those outcomes are reached and how they will do their part when implementing them. Each affected person needs to:

- feel some control over what's happening to them
- know that what they say matters
- feel appreciated for the contributions they are making
- have the opportunity for input
- understand that not everybody's recommendations can be implemented

The change management process steps:
1. Create the gap (need) to show the current way is not the best choice. Show the new way.

2. Create Attitudes towards the Advantages and Benefits of the new way. Help them see themselves already in possession of your product/service's Advantages and Benefits.

3. Talk about what will change and what won't change. Challenge them to defend what will change, especially how change solves problems and removes ill-effects of not changing.

4. Discuss support, training, supervision and other available resources.

5. Engage them in developing ways they will implement each change.

6. Agree on a clear path and plan to get the changes they now want.

Throughout this change management process, you will use the other skills you've learned in this book including the Competitor Analysis, FAB / TEA formula, Benefit Questions, Creating Attitudes, Active Listening Skills, Defusing Anger Skills, Saying "No" Creates Loss, Transition Sentences, Phrases of Persuasion and others.

Ensuring that each of the ten Buyer Beliefs is established with each decision-maker involved in the buying process will, by default, cover the main steps in the change management process.

Chapter 13: Skills Common to All Preempting Strategies

There are a few skill sets common to all preempting objections strategies. You will see these referenced, but not necessarily spelled out, throughout the rest of the book, so you might want to take a few minutes to familiarize yourself with the information now. Primary objectives:

- Understand the process to preempt objections you've confirmed exist with your competitor analysis.
- Use transition sentences to pave the way for the customer to accept your information.

You preempt objections by bringing them up and addressing them when it is most convenient for you, rather than waiting until the prospect brings them up, forcing you into a more defensive position of having to respond to them. The big difference is that you control when to bring them up.

You know which objections you need to preempt by looking at your competitor's perceived strengths (upper left quadrant 1) on the Competitor Analysis. And you know what information to use to neutralize these potential objections (upper right quadrant 2) or offset them in a trade-off situation (lower right quadrant 4). Common industry reputation and profession objections can also be added to the list of those to preempt.

Bringing up objections for discussion doesn't have to be scary. You don't have to call them objections or even consider them objections when you address them. Instead, think about them as common questions or concerns that you'd like to clarify.

The most common way to preempt objections is to introduce your supporting information with the objection stated as a question or concern and structured in a transition sentence. For example, "Many of our customers initially had a question (or concern) about _____, until they found out _____."

You could also select a time to address objections after you finished discussing information supportive of your position, and then transition to question or concern. For example, after providing the supportive information you could say, "And that's why we no longer have customer concerns about _____. That makes sense, doesn't it?"

Preemptive Strike Transition Sentences

The transition sentence is a diplomatic way to introduce sensitive topics where additional critical information is necessary or objections could occur.

Most people are not willing to change their minds but are willing to make a new decision based on new or redefined information. Use transition sentences whenever you are going to introduce different or opposing information. With transition sentences you can:

- Support without agreeing.
- Help them save face.
- Prevent arguments.
- Pull rather than push (Judo strategy).
- Prepare them to receive new information.

Transition sentence examples for preempting objections:

- "Before we go too much further, there are a couple of areas that I would like to address that without explanation could raise concern."
- "Many of our customers initially had a question about _____, until they found out _____."
- "A valid concern some of our customers have is with the _____. So to compensate we ___, _____, and ____. How do you see that working for you?"
- "There are _____ (number) areas your current supplier and our company are really good at providing." Now list them with a little discussion to clarify any concerns about your ability to do just as good a job in these areas as you competitor. This levels the playing field. Next, roll into your Research Questions guided by the topics of your USPs.
- "Some of our customers were initially concerned about the price differences until they started adding in all the hidden use costs that are exceptionally different from our offer. Let me briefly highlight some of those and show how our bottom-line value far exceeds the competition's top line low-pricing strategies."
- "By now, you're probably wondering how we're going to handle the ___ (name) concern that seems to plague the industry with this type of solution. Let's get right to how we do that so we can put it to rest."
- "It can be a hassle to change from one supplier to another so let me walk you through how we take care of that."
- "Let's focus for a moment not only on how we can meet this need but also how we can quantifiably

enhance that experience with our proprietary process to
_____, _____, and ____ (USPs)."

Now I'm sure you've heard some salespeople say, "If the prospect doesn't bring it up, I'm sure not going to." For many minor objections, that's probably not a bad strategy but it's not a good one either. It's so much easier to handle many of these routine "lack of information" types of objections with information presented in many ways from FAQs to highlighting it in brochures.

However, if it's a sale-stopping objection then you must bring it up. The worst thing that could happen is that the prospect doesn't voice it while you're there to respond. It could also be that some unknown person in the buying process brings it up, again while you're not there. Unless the decision-maker you've engaged now has the crucial information to provide the answer, you might not get the opportunity to give a response.

You know what objections to expect from your Competitor Analysis and field experience. You won't be able to prevent these because they already exist, but you can preempt them. This is a reality. Just as you'll do with your prevention strategies, it makes good sense to build your preemptions right into your sales process. It's always easier to address these issues when they are questions or concerns than it is waiting until you get the emotionally driven pushback of objections.

Chapter 14: Skills Common to All Responding Strategies

Objections will sometimes be raised before we can prevent or preempt them, and when that happens we need to be ready to respond. When an objection is voiced, it comes with emotional energy attached. Answering the objection without first defusing the emotion, could be counterproductive.

Emotions block a person's ability to think rationally. The stronger the emotion, the less rational they become. Even if you have a great answer, they may not be able to hear or comprehend what you're saying. You must first release the emotion to ensure your response will be received and accepted. This can be easily done using the Active Listening Skills (especially reflecting emotion) described below or using the Defusing Anger Skills.

Primary objectives:

- Understand the four step process to respond to objections.
- Use transition sentences to pave the way for the customer to accept your information.

Let's start with the four steps to respond to objections:

Four Steps to Responding

1. Listen
2. Transition

3. Answer
4. Confirm

The secret to responding to objections is to earn your right to be heard.

A Psychological Truth: *"If you sincerely try to understand another person's point of view first (not necessarily agree with it), then they become psychologically obligated to try to understand yours."*

You earn this right using your Active Listening Skills including:

- Acceptance Responses
- Repeating
- Paraphrasing content
- Reflecting emotion
- Ask Clarifying Questions
- Summarizing

Transition Sentence Magic

It is not uncommon that when prospective customers give you "pushback" as an objection, they will automatically brace themselves for your response. However, by first establishing your right to be heard with your Active Listening Skills, you're in a position to then "pull" them toward you (mental judo) by using transition sentences.

The transition sentences used for responding are similar to those used for preempting objections in the objectives they accomplish which are to:

- Support without agreeing.
- Help them save face.
- Prevent arguments.
- Pull rather than push (Judo strategy).
- Prepare them to receive new information.

Transition sentence examples for responding to objections:

- "Ordinarily, that would be my conclusion too, however . . ."
- "And that's exactly why I'm calling."
- "That's a good point and I'm glad you brought it up. When I first looked at this information, I came to the same conclusion, and then I found out . . ."
- "That's an important point I want to be sure to cover."
- "I understand how you feel because that's how I felt when I first came across this, and then I found out . . ."
- "That makes sense, and it also makes sense when you add . . ."
- "That's a valid objection to your application, so to compensate we . . ."
- "Under ordinary circumstances that would clearly apply, however, when we . . ."
- "That's what I said when I first heard about this, then I found out . . ."
- "I can understand how you could feel that way. In fact, several of my customers felt that way until they found out . . ."
- "And that's why we focus on providing a much better _____. Let me explain."
- "And . . ."

Test this. Take any objection you get and select a transition sentence from this list to start your answer. Next, make up some ridiculous statements and start a response with one of these transition sentences. For example, "Your house is upside down." Or "Your price is too high." As you can see, it doesn't matter what the person says, using your Active Listening Skills, and starting your answer with a transition sentence will pave the way for your answer to be given serious consideration.

Answer the Objection

Provide the missing or misunderstood information. You'll find this information in the upper right quadrant (Q2) of your Competitor Analysis. Once done, simply confirm agreement with your answer.

Confirm Your Answer

Get agreement that the new or reinterpreted information is valid and acceptable. You can do so by using standard Rhetorical Question Closes such as, "Isn't it?" "Wasn't it?" "Couldn't it?" and "Don't you agree?"

- "That makes sense, doesn't it?"
- "That's another possibility to consider, isn't it?"
- "This shows another way, don't you agree?"
- "And isn't this what you want to accomplish?"

You can also imply the rhetorical question. For example, just ending with "that makes sense," or, "that's a possibility," and then remaining quiet until they respond will accomplish the same objective.

Chapter 15: Answering the Unanswerable Objections

When the prospect raises an objection to which you have no straightforward answer or they want something you can't provide, you'll have to negotiate a trade-off to counter-balance what the prospect sees as a shortcoming. You do this by providing the customer with a choice between their objections or getting your Unique Selling Points. Therefore our primary objectives are to:

- Understand the basic purpose and structure of phrases of persuasion to set up the "trade-off" between what you don't have (their USPs) with what you do have that your competitors don't have (your USPs).
- Select and commit to memory two or three-phrase of persuasion.

The purpose of these phrases of persuasion is to provide the prospect with a choice between getting some of their needs filled one way or getting some other of their needs filled another way.

The structure is really a simple "this or that" question but using your USPs to provide your side of the equation.

If the one item you can't provide can be offset by one or more of your Unique Selling Points sufficient to tip the scales in your favor, then you have a trade-off negation that will work.

Your Unique Selling Points (USPs) can be strengthened appreciably in a trade-off negotiation when they have been fully quantified (FAB/TEA), and the Benefits Questions asked so that you already know the priority Business, Human, and Functional needs that must be filled. In this situation, you stand an outstanding chance of winning this negotiation.

Phrases of Persuasion

Before you start to create them on your own, take a look at few examples of standard formats for these specialized phrases.

Change the Basis of their Decision

Explanation: With this phrase of persuasion you get them to choose a different standard upon which to base their decision. Recall our earlier discussion on setting standards of legitimacy. The existence of one standard does not preclude the existence of another equally legitimate and more favorable standard.

Format: State the prospect's underlying needs (stated as needs, objectives, or goals) driving the sale, and then present the two standards in the form of a choice.

The priority _____ (needs, objectives, goals) for moving forward are _____, _____, and _____. The choice then really comes down to basing the decision on _____ (not so good standard) or _____ (better standard). Which makes better sense for your operation?

Plastic Container Example: The priority objectives are to reduce the overall budget in this area, get rid of the nasty hazardous job of changing the containers out, and present better optics for visiting customers. So now it comes down to choosing what to base the decision on; the lower cost at the top line that helps the budget but won't fill these critical needs, or focusing on a longer-term bottom-line impact and getting your needs in these areas filled. Which do you see as a better fit?"

Direct Comparison

Explanation: When the prospect points out something your competitor has that you do not, you'll want to acknowledge it by completely restating it (including reflecting any emotions) to firmly establish your right to be heard (see Active Listening Skills), and then ask how that choice will help them get their priority needs filled (problems solved by your USPs).

If you haven't already, you can use this opportunity to explore each of these USP areas in depth. Once done, your competitive position shifts in a very positive way.

Format: That's true; you do get _____ (restate what the prospect said). How does that help you get ____, ___, and ___ (Needs filled by your USPs)?

Note, don't use the word "but." If you do this might come too close to sounding like the very lame, "Yes, but" transition.

Plastic Container Example: "That's true; they do have a lower price per container and that does impact the top-line of your budget. How does that help you do away the replacement costs, rust stain cleaning costs, and the safety and image issues?"

Counter-Balancing Concerns

Explanation: The prospect expresses a concern about your offering compared to the competitors. Using the Active Listening Skills of repeating or paraphrasing, you let the prospect know you understand their concern. Next, let them know that you have a way to "counter-balance" their concerns by meeting related needs not currently being met and that you do this with your USPs.

Format: I know you're concerned about _____ (fully restate what they said). So we counter-balance that by making a bigger impact in meeting your high-priority needs in the areas of _____, _____, and _____ (needs met by USPs). How do you think that will work for you?"

Plastic Container Example: "I know you're concerned about the higher cost to get our containers. So we counter-balance that by focusing on creating a bigger impact directly to your bottom-line. We can do this by making our products so they don't have to be replaced so that you don't have to deal with the risks and nastiness if changing them out, and so that your visiting customers won't see rust stains. How do you see that approach being accepted by your company?"

Create Your Own Phrases of Persuasion

To help you better understand how these work and to help you create your own, you'll need three USPs and one customer request you can't directly fill or neutralize.

In each instance, you'll set up the trade-off negotiation with what you offer (that the competitor cannot) in positive terms and what the competitor offers (that you cannot) in less positive but not negative terms.

Usually, the phrase will be formulated as a question of "do you want this greater thing or that lesser thing?" For example, "Do you want to pay me now with a discount or pay me later with interest added?" Again, it's a simple "this or that" type question. Unless in your situation there is a compelling reason, it really doesn't matter which comes first the greater thing or the lesser thing.

If there is a way to mitigate or weaken the competitor's strong point, then include that in your phrase. For example, "We're really only looking at the difference in what they're charging and what we're charging rather than the whole amount. And when you add in the reduced costs associated with using it, we're not really too different, are we? So would the deciding factor be found in who can best help you meet your goals?" You could review the goals at this time or you could carry out the use costs over the term of the agreement as well to provide an even more enticing picture.

Your turn:
1. List three USPs (preferably as FABs).
2. List the one dreaded objection you can't directly neutralize.
3. Select a transition sentence from the previous chapter and write your "this or that" question.
4. Consider using three USPs to make it a "this or that, that, and that" (Objection or USP, USP, USP) question or even a "that, that, and that or this." (USP, USP, USP or Objection).

Part 2

Quick Start Guide

- Read the chapter opening remarks and general strategies for the category of objections in which your objection falls.
- Go to the specific objections you selected and choose from optional strategies provided those that would work best for you.
- Write the strategies you chose on Index (Flash) Cards with the objection stated on one side and the strategies you select on the lined side. Use different cards for the prevention, preemption and response strategies.
- Don't wait until you get index cards. Use the forms in the back of the book to learn the process of selecting the strategies that will work for you.

Return to Part 1

- Learn any of the skills that you don't already know but need in order to implement the recommendations you selected.
- Do a complete review of all the knowledge and skills provided in the first 79 pages to find the additional hidden gems that will boost your sales.

Chapter 16: Buyer Belief 1 – Need Exists

Common Objections in this Category

1. *Not Interested.*
2. *Already have someone.*
3. *We are satisfied with current supplier.*
4. *Don't need it.*
5. *We do it internally with our own people.*
6. *I can't use anymore _____.*

Category Overview

A need is a gap between where the prospective customer is now and where they want to be, or it's the gap between a problem and a solution. Therefore, the overall strategy is to establish the need by creating the gap.

You create the gap by calling the prospective customer's attention to their current situation (problem), and then painting them a picture of where they could be (solution) by having your product or service.

Understand that your prospect most likely already has someone meeting the functional needs your product or service meets. The needs you want to establish are for the unique capabilities you, your product/service and company can bring to the customer that your competitor cannot. These are your Unique Selling Points (USP). Often, these will fill needs prospects did not know they had or weren't aware there were solutions for them.

Earlier, you converted your USPs to FABs and learned that the missing Advantages and Benefits are the signs or symptoms (pain) that indicate the prospect doesn't have your USP's Feature. The solution to removing the pain is to get the USP Feature. Now you have both the problem and the solution defined. The gap has been created.

The "no need" objections are often first encountered during the initial contact and usually occur when we present or threaten to present. For example, if on an initial contact if we said, "The reason I am calling is to tell you about ____." Or "I would like to set up an appointment to show you ____." Then, you are clearly stating that you are going to take their time to present something, whether they need it or not. Therefore, you can expect to hear objections such as "not interested," or "already have someone," or "just send me your literature." These are smoke screen objections because the prospect does not realize s/he has needs.

You can prevent these objections by changing your approach and positioning strategy. For example, if you hear "just send me your literature," then you may want to open your conversation with, "The reason I'm calling is that I'd like to get you some written information about ____." So much for that objection!

To prevent the "not interested" objection, you could change your approach by opening the conversation with, "The reason I am calling is that I'd like to get you some written information about how our company has solved some costly and critical issues related to ___, ___, and ____." Fill in the blanks with USPs, or the missing Advantages and Benefits of your USPs' Features that are part of this person's job responsibilities. Continue with, "Is now a good time to quickly 'verify' some information?" Now take a slight pause and if no quick response to "go ahead," then ask, "Or would you like to set a telephone appointment for later today?" I usually recommend using two or three Unique Selling Points during your opening remarks. This gives you a wider range which will increase the probability that you'll hit on one that's important to him/her. Two or three hooks are usually better than one unless the one you have is indeed a showstopper.

If you get the go-ahead, you might ask, "Which of these areas, the ___, ___, or ___, is your greatest concern?" Then you know which area to explore first.

With this approach, instead of a 90% initial contact (phone or in-person) rejection rate, you'll flip this to a 90% acceptance rate.

Prevent, Preempt, and Respond Strategies for Individual Objections

1. Objection: *Not interested.*

> **When does it usually occur?** Initial contact.
> **Probable Cause:** Prospect does not believe a need exists.
> **Objective:** Establish a need.

Prevention Strategies:

1. A need is a gap between where the prospective customer is now and where they want to be, or it is the gap between a problem and a solution. Therefore, the overall strategy is to establish needs by creating the gaps. The needs you want to establish are the

Advantages and Benefits the unique capabilities you sell can bring the customer.

2. During your pre-call planning step, look for information that would suggest an obvious need you can fill, that your competitor cannot based on similar companies in your target market segment. Let your Unique Selling Points (USPs) guide your Research Questions. Use those areas as your initial topics of conversation.

3. Use your USP's Features to call your prospect's attention to solutions (Advantages and Benefits) they would want or need, given their decision-making role. For example, you might say on an initial contact, "The reason I'm calling is that I'd like to get you some written information about how our company has solved some costly and critical issues related to ___, ___, and ___ (USPs). Is now a good time to quickly verify some information, or do you want to set a telephone appointment for later today?"

4. Ask about the missing Advantages and Benefits that your USP's Feature provides. Ask about the costs associated with not having them. Connect your USP Feature that provides the solution, to its Advantages and Benefits that fill the need.

5. Always address commonly known problems your USPs can fix that are usually faced by decision-makers in similar roles.

6. Work with your Marketing Department to lay the foundation by identifying in your literature, problems only you can solve with your USPs.

Preemption Strategies:

1. You know that unless you can quickly and effectively draw the prospect's attention to a problem they need to

solve or to a solution that will help them achieve a goal with your USPs (relative to their decision-making role), the likelihood of getting "no need" type of objections is high. So you need to address that early on. Bring the objection up when it's most advantageous to you. If it's common enough, you could build it into your opening remarks.

2. Another strong preemption strategy would be to express high levels of enthusiasm for some unique capability you offer. Enthusiasm sells!

3. Go straight to the pain. Ask directly about your USPs missing Advantages and Benefits. For example, "How often are you seeing ____, ____, or ____?" "Are there any costs associated with that?" Using the plastic containers for an example, "How often do you have to buy new containers to replace those that rust?" "What is your monthly replacement budget?" Note that these are closed-ended questions that assume the events occur. They let you get a quantifiable number quickly to let the prospect feel the pain, build priority, and establish the initial support for ROI calculations. This strategy means three more categories of objections are on their way to being prevented (discomfort felt, priority, and ROI).

4. Work with your Marketing Department to develop literature and other promotional pieces to directly address (preempt) objections you get.

5. Use voice mail to leave a brief commercial to preempt the number one objection that otherwise would stop you cold. When you use voice mail always give your name (slowly), company and phone number at the beginning of any message. Give your 10-second elevator speech to preempt the specific objection. Be sure to add a hook to call you back (ask a question, say the next step, or

give a benefit). At the end of the call, say your name, company name, and phone number twice. Say these slowly and clearly.

Response Strategies:

1. "That's just what I said when I heard about this, then I found out why companies who ____ (state process you impact) could get ____ (state USP Benefit), which would solve ____ (state problem solved by your USP)."
2. "And that's exactly why I'm calling. Let me explain." (Explain, and then ask a qualifying or Research Questions to make sure you're on target).
3. "I can understand this isn't on your radar right now. We're also involved with ___ (state another USP's missing Advantages and Benefits that will move you to another opportunity within the company)." "Who would you recommend that I talk with about that?"
4. "Sounds like you've got too much on your plate to even consider something else, so let me do more research and get back to you once I've got more information for us to have a discussion. Thank you. Bye now." Get off the phone without letting the person tell you not to call anyone else in the company. Now call other decision-makers involved in the buying process.
5. "Yeah, I wasn't too interested in this one either until I compared it with a few alternatives on ____, ____, and ____ (USPs). That's when it became pretty clear to me that I needed to take a deeper look to see if I might have missed something that would make a big difference later. It's at least worth taking a couple of minutes to explore the possibility so we can feel confident ruling it out. That makes sense doesn't it?"

2. Objection: *Already have someone.*

> **When does it usually occur?** Initial contact.
> **Probable Cause:** Prospect believes their needs are getting met.
> **Objective:** Establish a need.

Prevention Strategies:

1. A need is a gap between where the prospective customer is now and where they want to be or it is the gap between a problem and a solution. Therefore, the overall strategy is to establish the need by finding or creating the gap. The size and importance of the gap determine its priority and value.

2. If what you're selling is an essential item or service, then most likely the prospect is doing business with someone else, so unless you can prevent or preempt it, you'll hear this objection a lot.

3. Focus the prospect's attention on the needs you can meet with your Unique Selling Points (USPs) Advantages and Benefits that make the functional need get met better, quicker, or cheaper.

4. You might make an initial call to find out who they're using so you can update your Competitor Analysis to ensure that when you call back you're prepared to orient to three strong Unique Selling Points (USPs).

5. During your approach/positioning opening remarks, give three USP Advantage and Benefit statements that you selected based on market segment, challenges common to that industry, and the decision maker's role. For example, "I'd like to get you some information about how our company is helping other companies in your industry to ___, ___, and to ___. Is now a good

time to quickly verify some information or, would you like to set a telephone appointment for later today?"

Preemption Strategies:

1. The approach/positioning strategy described above has proven time and again to be the most effective means of fending off this objection. If your company has a positive reputation and you're offering to get them some written information about how "your" company's R&D (research breakthrough, unique approach, and so on) generated the type results that you suspect your prospect would like to have, then it doesn't matter to the prospect if they have someone else. They'd still like to review the information.

2. Notice how I said; "get" you some information in this example. That leaves it open to mailing them some written information, attaching a PDF file to an e-mail, taking them to a website while they are on the phone with you to show them the information, conducting a demonstration, and many other ways to accomplish the goal of "getting" them the information.

3. Use the rapport building technique of finding a common ground to make the point that you both experienced products like cell phones, computers, or cars and sought out new ones to enhance the Advantages and Benefits you received. Talk about how much these have changed and how much more you can do with them. Emphasize that by making the changes they were able to get more of the Advantages and Benefits they wanted. Then transition to your product, and how they might profit from looking at a different supplier.

Response Strategies:

1. Get the opportunity to tell your story. This is a great strategy.

   Quickly Find the Pain: "Makes sense that you would. And that leads me to a quick question. We (or our customers) are seeing a lot of change in the areas of ___, ___, and ___ (USPs); I'm assuming your operation would be experiencing this too. What are your greatest concerns with ___ (missing advantages and benefits of one of the USPs)?"

   Create Urgency for Meeting: Use the FAB/TEA Value Selling process to briefly explore the associated costs to build the priority need to get some form of resolution. Flow from USP to USP, and then close on a phone or in-person appointment to explore these areas in greater depth.

   Set the Meeting: "So if you're seeing ___, ___, and ___ (signs they don't have your USPs) and given that the costs we've identified so far, then we're both seeing a few red flags that say we need to explore this further. I can do that quickly. How soon would you like to get this done? What's your schedule look like this week? Do you have a couple preferred times?"

2. "And that's exactly why I'm calling. Sometimes our company's primary role turns out to be augmenting critical areas not getting met through regular channel suppliers such as ___ and ___ (USPs). Would it be alright for me to get you some written information about how those areas typically affect ___ operations? Or we could, within the next couple of minutes, get a pretty good idea about how much this is affecting your operation."

3. Objection: *We're satisfied with our current supplier.*

When does it usually occur? Initial contact.
Probable Cause: Prospect does not believe a need exists.
Objective: Establish a need.

Prevention Strategies:

1. The overall strategy is designed to get the prospect to recognize that there might be weaknesses in their current supplier's product, service, or business strategy by pointing out your Unique Selling Points.
2. During your pre-call planning, do a quick update of your Competitor Analysis to make sure you know your strengths against this competitor's weaknesses for prospects in your target market segment.
3. During your opening remarks, state that you want to "get them some written information" about how your company has solved costly and critical issues related to ___, ___, and ___." State three areas where you are strong (USPs), your competitor is weak, and typical customers in this market segment have needs.
4. Get permission to proceed, and then ask questions targeted toward discovering needs. An example of doing this would be, "Is now a good time to quickly verify some information or should we set a phone appointment for later today?" With an "okay" from the prospect, you might ask a question such as, "What are your greatest concerns related to ____ (missing USP)?" Or you could continue with your USP guided Research Questions.
5. Plastic container example: "What are your greatest concerns about the risks your employees face when

transferring product from the rusting container to a new one?"

Preemption Strategies:

1. Know this one is coming, spoken or not! It can be a hassle for prospective customers to change suppliers, so you're working with an existing inertia that will need to be overcome. Bring out the "big bang" Benefits up front. Don't hold back. But, before you do, make sure your credibility is clearly established first. For example, "We're the company (firm, organization) that _____." Insert what you're known for, or would like to be known for.

2. Similar to the previous objection (*already have someone*), the strategy here is to get the prospect to realize that they have changed suppliers on any number of products and services in the past and have benefited from it. Talk about how happy you were with the car, computer, phone, and so on, when you first got it, and then how that changed as new capabilities you wanted became available but the supplier you were happy with couldn't provide. Ask, "So what do you do when you really want something you can't get from your current supplier?" Now transition to your Unique Selling Point's missing Advantages and Benefits. For example, "What are your greatest concerns about not having the ability to ___ (missing USP)?"

Response Strategies:

1. Get the opportunity to tell your story. This is a great strategy.

   Quickly Find the Pain: "Makes sense that you would. And that leads me to a quick question. We (or our customers) are seeing a lot of change in the areas of ___, ___, and ___ (USPs); I'm assuming your operation would be experiencing this too. What are your greatest concerns with ___ (missing advantages and benefits of one of the USPs)?"

   Create Urgency for Meeting: Use the FAB/TEA Value Selling process to briefly explore the associated costs to build the priority need to get some form of resolution. Flow from USP to USP, and then close on a phone or in-person appointment to explore these areas in greater depth.

   Set the Meeting: "So if you're seeing ___, ___, and ___ (signs they don't have your USPs) and given that the costs we've identified so far, then we're both seeing a few red flags that say we need to explore this further. I can do that quickly. How soon would you like to get this done? What's your schedule look like this week? Do you have a couple preferred times?

2. "Great, it's not easy to find a good supplier in this business, who are you currently using? When you think about ___, (USP) what are your greatest concerns?"

3. "That's why I'm calling. There are some major changes in ___ and in ___ (state areas of greatest change related to your Unique Selling Points), and I would like to get you some written information about how we're seeing these issues impact your industry's ability to ___. Is now a good time to quickly verify some information?"

4. **Objection:** *Don't need it.*

> **When does it usually occur?** Initial contact.
> **Probable Cause:** Prospect does not believe a need exists.
> **Objective:** Establish a need.

Prevention Strategies:

1. Often, the need is already being met. So you won't get far going head-to-head against the competitor. Go instead for "how" the need is being met. Look for the areas that you excel (USPs) and your competitor is weak. Look at your Competitor Analysis to see whether there are other areas you could explore.
2. Remember, "Do Nothing" is a competitor. The prospect may not know they have a need or think it's so far down the list of priorities; they are not planning to do anything. Conduct a Competitor Analysis against "Do Nothing" to find ways to create a need.
3. During your pre-call planning, look for information that would suggest an obvious need based on similar companies in this market segment. Create the gap with your USP's missing Advantages and Benefits. Sometimes a sliver of a crack is all you need to build it into something monumental using Benefit Questions.
4. Review your Competitor Analysis for areas to orient the prospect during your opening remarks. For example, "I'd like to get you some information on how our company has solved some costly and critical issues related to ___, ___, and ___ (USPs). Is now a good time to quickly verify some information (slight pause to see if they answer, and then if not) or, should we set a phone appointment for later in the day?"

Preemption Strategies:

1. When the decision-maker doesn't believe a need exists, you must either find the pain (missing Advantages and Benefits) or create a picture that makes doing it your way so much better that it creates a Benefit deficit. Just look at all the new cell phones, watches, shoes, navigation tools, and other things that make our lives so much better that we'll spend a lot of money to get them. Position what you sell this way.

2. Present a unique capability, and then offer to show how quickly it pays for itself (financially, subjectively, or emotionally). You could initially use your company's research facts and figures, if available, to provide some shock value. Or you could use standards of legitimacy to provide examples.

Response Strategies:

1. "That may be true. However, let's compare the two on what you're currently spending annually; to what you would be spending if you decided to use products with these capabilities. Then you would have the cost-benefit information on which to base your decision. That makes sense, doesn't it?"

2. "Yeah, a lot of us thought that too, and then we found out that we could ___, ___, and ___ in a fraction of the time, with none of the frustration. Paid for itself many times over the first time we used it."

5. **Objection:** *We do it internally with our own people.*

When does it usually occur? Initial contact.
Probable Cause: Prospect does not believe a need exists.
Objective: Establish a need.

Prevention Strategies:

1. This strategy relies on learning about "how" they do it internally. Look for the holes in the process they use that you could fill in all the areas you impact including their products, services, critical processes, business plan, strategic initiatives, and their competitive selling environment (see Research Questions).

2. During your initial research of the company, find out who you compete against. Internal competition must also be analyzed. Map the processes the company (and your internal competition) uses (Research Questions) to find the holes in what they do. You might even want to draw a flowchart. Your initial sales objective is to go after a "piece of the pie."

3. If "doing it internally" is common for your target market, then you'll need to augment your strategy with involvement with their trade and professional organizations. Remember that the people who do what you do internally for the prospect learn how to do it somewhere. They often rely on the industry experts they network with at their trade or professional organization. Find out how they keep up to date. If it's a trade or professional organization, then get involved. Consider co-presenting with a customer, writing articles for publication, and serving on select committees

(publication and membership are the two with the highest payoff).

4. Focus your introductory comments in areas where you are strong and they are weak. State how you like to work with internal departments because they can leverage what you offer to multiply the results and everyone looks good.

5. Have at least one or two USPs that you know few, if any, internal departments would be able to do. Focus your introductory comments in these areas.

Preemption Strategies:

1. When you update your Competitor Analysis, you'll know that you've got an internal resource competing with you, but this probably won't be the first time this has happened to you or anyone else in your company. Talk with the people in your company about what they like and don't like about accessing third-party resources, or about salespeople calling to offer services to do what they do. Ask what they would see as the best approach a salesperson could use when contacting them.

2. Competing or supporting can come down to a state of mind. Know where you can help (Competitor Analysis and Research Questions) and know where they need to feel secure in their core areas (Competitor Analysis and Research Questions), and then focus on the "support" and "fill-in" strategies.

3. For many internal groups, the resources they need to do their jobs often reach the "make or buy" decision several times a year and sometimes, several times on the same project at different points. Be their "go to" resource for information. Make sure you continue to

network higher into the organization so you become a known asset.

Response Strategies:

1. "You are very fortunate to get in-house support in these areas. Would you know offhand whether they outsource jobs in the areas of ___, ___ or ___ (USPs)? Who is most affected by those areas? Who would I talk to in that department?"
2. "That's great. We're the company that provides support in the areas of ___, ___, and ____ (USPs). Let me transfer to them to talk about any low cost or no cost immediate needs they might have that we could help them with. Who would you recommend I talk with?"

6. Objection: *I can't use anymore ___.*

>   **When does it usually occur?** Initial contact.
>   **Probable Cause:** Prospect does not believe a need exists.
>   **Objective:** Establish a need.

Prevention Strategies:

1. The overall game plan is helping the customer prepare for the future when they will need more (of whatever). For example, imagine a chart tracking consumption increasing and available inventory steadily decreasing. At some point in time, the inventory line will go below the usage line and the company will need to replenish its supply. Some companies try to replenish inventory in a way that it will keep pace with demand while other companies use oversupply situations with their

suppliers to buy inventory at steeply discounted prices. Understand your prospective customer's business model.

2. During your research of the industry and talking with your customers, you can determine standard consumption rates and standard inventory levels. This will help you with timing and planning issues with prospective customers.

3. Be sensitive to industry conditions to head off oversupply issues leading to returns or steep price discounts.

4. One top sales professional I know sells fasteners. Many of his customers allow him into their inventory rooms to make sure they keep a previously agreed inventory count available based on current and projected rates of consumption. Get invited to review inventory needs. Share your industry expertise with your buyers. Build your relationships so the buyers come to rely on your expertise.

Preemption Strategies:

1. If you suspect they may be overstocked, you can preempt this objection by asking directly about their consumption rate, then emphasize and go into a future planning mode based on their business model.

2. Sometimes you'll pick up a pattern with certain competitors where they have a deliberate strategy of keeping their customers just on the high side of inventory requirements. One way to deal with this is to talk with the customer about the cost of money losses (tied up in inventory), inventory insurance costs, taxes on finished products on the shelf, warehousing costs, and other financial hits and risks they're taking by

getting pulled into buying high levels of inventory. If you can offer "just in time" deliveries, then you have a good chance of getting in the door without the objection coming up. Become your prospective customer's consultant and ear to the ground information source.

Response Strategies:

1. "Well, I can tell the timing isn't right now. What is your consumption rate so we can set our next conversation at a more appropriate time? What slowed the consumption rate from the planned rate? Okay, so I'll make a note to include a restocking paragraph to make sure you don't get stuck with inventory you can't use. Thank you and I've scheduled to call you on the ___ to set our meeting. What part of the day is the best time to reach you?"

2. "That's a good point and I'm glad you brought that up. Ordinarily, keeping inventory matched with consumption is a good plan, however, some of my customers are also taking this opportunity to buy select overstocked inventory at steep discounts. I think it might make sense to see which items might work for you with this type of strategy, especially if we can get some clear indications of when consumption will pick up."

3. "So that's a great reason for us to talk about "just in time" inventory strategies now before things start moving again. I think we can help you free up dollars you've got tied up in your inventory. Makes sense to do this now, doesn't it? When would be a good time for us to get together for a quick orientation and planning session?"

Chapter 17: Buyer Beliefs 2 and 3 – Responsibility and Authority

Common Objections in this Category

7. *My boss won't authorize anything.*
8. *It will never get through the system.*
9. *I have to consult with _____.*
10. *That's not my area.*
11. *That has value, but not for me.*
12. *Home office requires we use _____.*
13. *We have to use your competitor.*
14. *He/she isn't here anymore.*

Category Overview

Frequently, people who share in the responsibility to find and evaluate products often share authority for participating in purchasing them. As such, the strategies and tactics for both Buyer Beliefs (Responsibility and Authority) are so similar, that they are combined here to avoid repetition.

These objections can often be prevented by asking appropriate clarifying questions to determine how the prospect's company makes decisions, the people involved in the process and why they're involved. Look at your customer profiles. If other customers of a similar size and industry have certain people involved in the decision-making process, then you'd be better off assuming their counterparts in this company will have some say in the final selection.

Key Decision-Making Roles

1. **Final Authority:** ROI
2. **Specifier:** Performance specifications to meet functional needs and cost-justification
3. **Negotiator:** Feature to Price ratio.
4. **Consumer / End User:** Interested in user-friendliness.
5. **Coach / Mentor / Sponsor:** Inside the buying loop.
6. **Recommenders:** Usually outside the buying loop.

One person can play up to five decision-making roles or you may have two or more people carrying out one role.

Decision-makers are also biased.

- **Champions:** Can sell for you internally when you're not around.
- **Favorable:** Would prefer you.
- **Neutral:** Neither for you nor against you.
- **Unfavorable:** Would prefer someone other than you.
- **Blocker:** Champion of your competitor or doesn't like something about your company.

Prevent, Preempt, and Respond Strategies for Individual Objections

7. Objection: *My boss won't authorize anything.*

> **When does it usually occur?** Early closing after the presentation.
> **Probable Cause:** Buyer does not believe s/he has authority.

Objective: Identify people who play the various decision-making roles.

Prevention Strategies:

1. Identify from your lead source (referral, directory, or network), the people who (by title or position) would most likely be in the different decision-making roles.
2. During your initial contact with the receptionist, you could also ask, "Who *are* the people, who would make decisions about the products/services used in ___ (specify area)." Interact with the highest-level person you can reach.
3. Always develop everyone you can into a coach. Start this type relationship with the hard to resist question, "Can you please help me?"
4. From your experience, you could ask about decision-makers typically involved in buying what you sell to make sure they're in the mix. You can also make sure you're getting the right person by asking questions about each role. For example, "Who would make the decisions about performance specifications?" Or "Who would decide the necessary level of return on investment before a product/service could be preapproved for the purchasing department to order?"
5. When closing out this step with someone who could give you this objection say, "I guess one of our next steps will be to do a thorough cost justification so you'll have the numbers you'll need to provide to your manager. What is the approval process for this type of project?"

Preemption Strategies:

1. Quantify (financial, subjective, and emotional) what it costs not to have the Advantages and Benefits of your Unique Selling Points' Features.
2. Identify the other decision-makers. "In addition to you, who else would be involved with deciding ____ (name the types of decisions to be made such as, ROI, performance specifications, and ease of use)?"
3. Ask the decision-maker you're interacting with how getting your USPs would benefit the other decision-makers. Guide them by asking about specific decision-makers.
4. Ask how something like this could be worked into the budget.
5. Lay out a plan for you to meet with the other decision-makers to continue to gather information.
6. The stronger your quantifying questions, the more sense of urgency you will create. The greater the number of areas where you can find issues (missing USPs), the greater the subjective, emotional, and financial sense of urgency you will create.
7. Consider that you most likely do not have a line-item in your budget for a new tire for your car, but if you were to get a flat and destroy the tire, what would you do? Most likely you would move money from one area of your budget to another to get a new tire, wouldn't you? Find the decision-maker(s) responsible for all the budgets you impact. They can move money from one budget to another. Help them find the money.

Response Strategies:

1. "I understand, my boss won't authorize anything either unless I have some pretty strong cost-justification for at least reviewing a project. Is that about where s/he is right now?"
2. "I can certainly understand how you feel, I'm in the same position, but if this makes sense and we can cost-justify it, what other information do you think we need to take it to the next step?"
3. "I wouldn't expect him to at this step in the process. We've got to first make sure the return on investment will be large enough, soon enough, and certain enough for him to feel confident enough to release the funds. I suspect that if you're operationally set up like my other customers, then I would estimate that you're currently spending, and have budgeted, at least three to five times the money we would need if you were to use our products and services. So if we can cut your budget in half for this item and use part of that money to make the change, then I think you'll agree that it's worth taking a few minutes to explore the possibility, don't you?"
4. "Won't authorize anything?" Now clarify the circumstances under which authorization can be obtained.

8. Objection: *It will never get through the system.*

When does it usually occur? After your presentation.
Probable Cause: Prospect doesn't believe s/he has enough authority to move the project forward or is unsure how to proceed.
Objective: Identify the key decision-makers in this sale and create coaches and champions.

Prevention Strategies:

1. In general, you'll need to identify the decision-makers by the type of decisions they make. Remember there could be more than one person in a role and there could be one person in several roles. Create coaches of the decision-makers you are interacting with to get support to interact with the other decision-makers.
2. Identify from your lead sources (referral, directory, or network), who, by title or function, would most likely be in the different decision-making roles. See the profile characteristics of accounts in this market segment and size company to identify the titles of high probability decision-makers.
3. Ask questions about how your products/services will benefit the key decision-makers.
4. While setting the agenda for the next meeting, say, "This will require input from several people in different parts of your company, so what we'll want to do is identify who needs to be involved and when they should be brought into the loop. I could see that we need to meet with ___ (specify role/person/title) during our next one or two meetings, who else do you think we should include in that meeting?"
5. Continue to work with the decision-makers you have access to, so you can develop Coaches and Champions to move the purchase through the system.

Preemption Strategies:

1. Whenever you see that you don't have all the relevant decision-makers identified and in the room, don't make a final presentation. If you have to do something, make a tentative or draft presentation to get most details

handled. Allow time during your presentation to get any information that you're missing. This could include cost justification, specifications, buying process, timelines, decision-makers, next steps and so on.

2. Without the critical sales information you need to complete the steps in your sales process, it's not the time to ask for the order. Identify the steps in your sales process that should be completed before you ask for an order. You want to make sure the order will not get canceled because you missed a step along the way.

3. Ask a lot of Benefit Questions to create Coaches and Champions.

Response Strategies:

1. "Under normal circumstances, I would be in total agreement with you. However, based on what we've discovered, we're going to have to take our findings to the next level, or we could be put into a position of having to answer some tough questions when this comes to light and we didn't at least let them know. We need a solid strategy to make sure what we have gets interpreted accurately. So, I recommend we first verify ___, next we can ___ (continue to build a plan)."

2. "That's the next question I've got. What are the steps in your process, who are people we've yet to interview, how do you set priorities on budgeting, and given that this is something that will benefit each of you, how can we work together to realize those Benefits?"

9. Objection: *I have to consult with ___.*

> **When does it usually occur?** After presentation.
> **Probable Cause:** Prospect does not believe he/she has full authority to move forward.
> **Objective:** Identify the buying influences.

Prevention Strategies:

1. Identify from your lead sources (referral, directory, or network), who, by title or function, would most likely be in the different decision-making roles.
2. In your initial interview, identify the people making decisions about your sale. Make sure the person you are talking with becomes your Coach.
3. The person becomes your Coach when you ask them solid diagnostic questions using the Research Questions, FAB / TEA formula, and Benefit Questions. Target some of your Benefit Questions toward other decision-makers. Once they can confidently describe the Benefits other decision-makers will get, they are now in a position to champion your cause.

Preemption Strategies:

1. Identify the decision-makers as an early step in learning how your prospective customer buys. Knowing others will need to be consulted, a part of your interaction with this decision-maker is to recruit them as a coach. The quickest and easiest way to create a coach is with the magic words, "Would you help me please?" Very few people can turn that request down.

2. Ask your Benefit Questions in a way that will help you identify other key decision-makers. For example, "Who would be most interested in the ROI this will bring?"

Response Strategies:

1. "It sounds as if we're moving forward. What type of decision will ___ be making about this purchase? Who else will be involved? What types of decisions will they make? Let's make sure you have the information you need to answer any questions they might have." For example, "Mr. Jones will be determining whether the return is worth the investment, so let's work out a brief cost-benefit analysis to highlight the return, then we can go to work on finding the appropriate references."

2. "Good point and thank you for reminding me to ask about the others involved in the decision process. Would you help me please and guide me through the process that we'll need to navigate to make sure the right people are included?"

10. Objection: *That's not my area.*

When does it usually occur? After the initial introduction of your products/services.
Probable Cause: Prospect does not believe he/she has the responsibility or authority to move forward.
Objective: Identify the buying influences.

Prevention Strategies:

1. Find the decision-makers. Recall that you've got six different decision-making roles involved, even if one person makes five of the decisions. You'll know which

role they're in by the questions they ask. For example, if they ask about specifications then they are in the Specifier role. If they ask about cost justification, they are again in the Specifier role. But if they ask about return on investment, then they have switched to the Final Authority role. At this point, it would be important to clarify if they are a part of the Final Authority role or are they getting this information on behalf of the Final Authority.

2. Sometimes we do end up talking with a person not involved in a sales opportunity. This happens a lot during networking events. The general strategy then is to first create a Coach and then ask for referrals to the correct decision-makers.

3. Identify from your lead sources (referral, directory, or network), who, by title or function, would most likely be in the different decision-making roles.

4. During your initial contact with the receptionist, ask who would be involved in making the decisions about the products/services used in ___ .

5. After your initial diagnostic interview, you would ask who the other decision-makers are that would need to be involved in the approval process.

Preemption Strategies:

1. As a routine part of your sales process, identify the key decision-makers and develop Coaches along the way.

2. Ask your Benefit Questions in a way that will help you identify other key decision-makers. For example, "Who would be most interested in the ROI this will bring?"

3. Ask, "Could you help me please?" This "hard to resist question" will help the person become your Coach. Then ask, "Who *are* the people involved in making

decisions regarding ___?" Ask, "Whose budget would be most affected?" Ask, "Can you help me get in to see ___?" If hesitation, then ask, "Or perhaps I could mention that we talked?"

Response Strategies:

1. "Thank you for letting me know. Who *are* the people to talk to? Who would you recommend I contact?" When is the best time to catch ___ and ___? Before I go, do you have any thoughts in this area that would help your company?"
2. "Okay, that's good to know. Who should I talk with? Could you help me contact them? I would really appreciate that. Is there anything I should know about him/her before I see them?"

11. Objection: *That has value, but not for me.*

> **When does it usually occur?** After presentation or elevator speech.
>
> **Probable Cause:** Prospect does not have the responsibility for the primary area of value your product/service offers.
>
> **Objective:** Identify the correct buying influences.

Prevention Strategies:

1. As with the previous objection, you'll need to find the decision-makers in each of the six roles. If not, as a default thought, consider them favorable to your competitor.
2. Another possibility with this objection is that the prospect is the right decision-maker but doesn't see the value. This would mean that you're trying to solve a

problem that the prospect doesn't know he/she has. In this case, you'll need to be sure to conduct your diagnostic interview by asking the prospect about their greatest concerns about not having the Advantages and Benefits of your Unique Selling Points. Once established, then you can confirm the existence of a problem and start to quantify the value of the solution (what it costs the prospect not to have the Advantages and Benefits).

3. Identify from your lead sources (referral, directory, or network), who, by title or function, would most likely be in the different decision-making roles. Identify who needs to be involved and when they should be brought into the loop.

4. During your initial contact with the receptionist, ask who the people are that would be involved in making the decisions about specifying your product/service.

5. Ask the prospect what Benefits they and those involved would receive from using your products/services (Benefit Questions).

6. During your research, determine the areas in the prospect's company where you have the greatest impact. Use your USPs to guide your Research Questions.

7. Establish the existence of a problem that you can solve with your Unique Selling Points (FAB / TEA formula).

8. Quantify (financial, subjective, emotional) the value of the Benefits to the decision-maker to help them see that it does have value to them (FAB / TEA formula).

Preemption Strategies:

1. As a routine part of your sales process, identify the key decision-makers and develop coaches along the way.

The quickest and easiest way to create a coach is with the magic words, "Would you help me please?" Very few people can turn that request down.

2. Explore the existence of problems by determining whether there is any pain over not having the Advantages and Benefits of your Unique Selling Points or whether there is anything to be gained by having them. Quantify the results financially and subjectively.

Response Strategies:

1. "That's an observation that many of my customers initially made until they found out _____." Now explain its value. If this is not the right person, then find out who that would be and when would be the best time to contact them.

2. "Thank you, who in your organization do you think would Benefit from this?"

3. "Let me back up a moment and ask you about _____." Now ask your diagnostic questions about pain or gain about your Unique Selling Point's Advantages and Benefits.

12. Objection: *Home office requires that we use _____.*

When does it usually occur? After the initial introduction of your product/service.
Probable Cause: Prospect does not believe he/she has the authority to move forward.
Objective: Identify the buying influences.

Prevention Strategies:

1. Find the decision-makers in the home office. As a routine part of your sales process, identify the key decision-makers and develop Coaches along the way. The quickest and easiest way to develop a Coach is with the magic words, "Would you help me please?" Very few people can turn that request down.
2. Identify from your lead sources (referral, directory, or network), who, by title or function, would most likely be in the different decision-making roles. Identify who needs to be involved and when they should be brought into the loop.
3. During your initial contact with the receptionist, ask, who "are" the people involved in making decisions about _____.
4. Ask the prospect what Benefits they and the other decision-makers will receive from using your products/services.

Preemption Strategies:

1. You'll probably notice that several of your customers of this size and industry have some central buying process. Confirm this. Then ask how they get something they need in front of the right decision-makers at their home office.
2. Create Coaches and Mentors to guide you.
3. If you also recognize that your offering is substantially different from what the competitor offers, you might explore how they buy these types of things not on the national contract.

Response Strategies:

1. "Thank you for letting me know that. Who are the people I should contact there? Do you have their phone number? Just to clarify, the agreement they made, what leeway do you have for items not provided by that supplier?" If yes, then orient to areas where you are strong and the competitor is weak and ask the prospect about the concerns they have in these areas. This will either allow you to move forward or will give you the information you need to move forward at the home office.

2. "We like national contracts as well. Thank you. Before we move to that phase of the process, I wonder if you could help me, please. I'd like to explore the major differences in what we offer with what you have on your national contract. That way, we would all know whether this is something we need to pursue now. By the way, do you know when that contract comes up for negotiation?"

3. "Thank you for letting me know. I wonder if you could help me, please. Who are the decision-makers in your home office that people in our company would be able to contact?"

13. Objection: *We have to use your competitor.*

> **When does it usually occur?** After the initial introduction of your products/services.
> **Probable Cause:** Prospect does not believe he/she has the authority to move forward.
> **Objective:** Identify the buying influences over the type and length of the agreement.

Prevention Strategies:

1. Usually, these types of objections are actual "conditions" resulting from some form of partnering agreement made at the highest levels of the organization. These agreements are exclusive to a single or small group of competitors. They are usually a result of the quality process in which customer and vendor partner agree to share in cost savings, do team building activities, get their computer systems to talk to each other, and so on. It's a sizable investment for both the customer and the suppliers. However, about every three to five years, these agreements come up for negotiated renewal and exploration with other vendors if there is the possibility that the customer could Benefit more.

2. A consistently successful approach is to intensely focus on your differentiating factors so your solution can be painted as something different than what's being offered in the national contract. Recognize that most of these contracts have exceptions where specialty types of products that meet specific needs, not covered under the national contract, can be locally sourced and readily purchased.

3. Find the decision-makers. Identify from your lead sources (referral, directory, or network), who, by title or function, would most likely be in the different decision-making roles.

4. During your initial contact with the receptionist, ask who the people are making the decisions about what you sell.

5. After your initial diagnostic interview, you would ask who else will need to be involved in the approval process.

6. Ask your Benefit Questions in a way that will help you identify other key decision-makers. For example, "Who would be most interested in the ROI this will bring?

7. Find out the timing of these agreements and any available back doors. Develop internal Coaches and Mentors to guide you. Continue to focus on communicating your Unique Selling Points.

8. These types of agreements do come apart for many reasons such as a change in key staff (supplier or customer), sudden quality issues, personality conflicts, business model changes, product discontinuation, and so on. That's why you need people (coaches and champions) inside the prospect's company who will let you know when something is about to disrupt the agreement.

Preemption Strategies:

1. Your customer profile and industry knowledge will often clue you into these types of agreements. Given the existence of these contracts in your target market, this should become one of your early qualifying questions.

2. Once you've established the existence of these agreements, then your next step would be to find out the degree of flexibility, how something can be purchased off contract, the timing for renegotiation, decision-makers involved and so on.

3. Work to have extensive financial quantification available from other customers.

4. Identify business needs or strategic initiatives, such as safety, that you can position yourself around.

5. Get a "piece of the pie" with any of your products/services to make sure you're on the list of

companies to negotiate with when the contract comes up for renewal.

Response Strategies:

1. "Have to use our competitors?" Learn more about this situation. Guide as necessary to get a reason based explanation, not an emotion infused defense.
2. "Thank you for that information. That is a position I would like to be in, and I guess, so would your salespeople. Could you tell me how that came about?"
3. "Just to clarify the agreement they made. If _____ (current supplier) isn't able to meet your needs, what leeway do you have?" If some, then move to ask about concerns related to your USPs. Quantify everything. Then find out when the agreement is up for renewal and the decision-makers involved so you can call at the appropriate time.
4. "Well that's disappointing but let's push on." Explore other products and services you have to sell, find the decision-makers and get introductions. At the end, circle back around to the national contract and explore possibilities, flexibilities, timing and so on. Your objective would then be to position your company to get the opportunity to be a serious contender when the contract comes up again. Much of that will depend on how much you can learn about the customer and then modify your offering and how you do business to match their ever-changing needs.

14. Objection: *He/she isn't here anymore.*

> **When does it usually occur?** When you ask for a specific person.
> **Probable Cause:** Person isn't there.
> **Objective:** Identify the buying influences.

Prevention Strategies:

1. Sometimes the prospect contact lists we use are really bad. Wrong numbers, people in different roles, or gone from the company altogether. Then again, we should anticipate at least a 30% turnover in two or three years. People leave, switch jobs, are transferred, and get promoted. That can be a good thing, especially if the person you're contacting has blocked you in the past.

2. Identify from your lead sources (referral, directory, or network), who, by title or function, would most likely be in the different decision-making roles.

3. During your initial contact with the receptionist, ask who the people are that would be making the decisions about those products/services used in _____. If you asked, who "is," then you'd get one person, possibly someone in the Purchasing Department. That may be a good thing if you don't know anyone in the company. They can be a great source for getting referrals to Specifiers inside their company.

4. After your initial diagnostic interview, you would ask who else will need to be involved in the approval process. Offer names to check out their role.

Preemption Strategies:

1. Some prospect lists are notoriously bad. If you get one of those, start with the basic interview questions. Ask if the person on the list is still involved with decisions regarding (your product). If you get the "he's not here anymore" or "she's been transferred to wherever and not in this role." type response, then you have the opportunity to ask who now makes those decisions and who else is involved.

2. If they are still with the company, contact them and turn them into a Coach by asking the magic question, "Would you help me please?"

3. Sometimes when all else fails, ask to speak with someone in purchasing. Turn that person into a Coach and go from there.

4. Ask your Benefit Questions in a way that will help you identify other key decision-makers. For example, "Who would be most interested in the ROI this will bring?"

5. In some industries, where decision-making roles are constantly changing, people in the Purchasing Department are your best source to learn who's involved in which projects. Getting a referral from someone in the Purchasing Department helps you get to those people in the Specifier roles directly and quickly.

Response Strategies:

1. "S/he was involved in the decisions related to _____, who would now handle that responsibility?" Find out, and then ask who else would be involved in making decisions about those product/services used in _____. Ask when is the best time to contact them. Get

connected to the highest-level person in the buying loop.

2. "Can you tell me who took his place?" If yes, then get connected, if not, go to the previous employee's department for guidance. If no, contact the Purchasing Department to find the right decision-makers and to develop Coaches.

Chapter 18: Buyer Belief 4 – Discomfort Felt

Common Objections in this Category

15. Just send me your literature.
16. Don't have time to discuss this now.
17. No one paying attention to this area.
18. We'll muddle through.
19. It's too much hassle.
20. We won't use it.

Category Overview

If a prospective customer doesn't feel any discomfort from not having a "need" or "want" filled, then it becomes of little importance to change what they are doing now.

Learning about your prospect's business is necessary to know where to look for the pain or where you could quantifiably improve their situation. Let your Unique Selling Points (USP) guide your Research Questions to explore for the missing Advantages and Benefits provided by your Unique Selling Points (USP) Feature:

1. **Prospect's products and services**: USPs related to helping make the prospect's products and services better. USPs related to how their sales strategy may be affected by your products and services.
2. **Prospect's critical processes**: USPs related to how they make their money. Map the workflow process to see the critical areas where what you sell impacts their

ability to make money: increase profits, reduce costs, strengthen image, and reduce risks.

3. **Prospect's business plan**: USPs related to the prospect's strategic initiatives, goals, buying cycles, budgeting, and so on.

By asking questions about the missing Advantages and Benefits of your Unique Selling Points, you will raise the awareness in the prospect's mind of how it would feel not to have this need filled. The more missing Advantages and Benefits of your Unique Selling Points you can address, the greater the discomfort they feel. The more you can quantify the pain subjectively and financially, the greater the discomfort and the stronger the motivation will be to get the Benefits.

However, to establish this Buyer Belief, you need only to bring awareness to the discomfort they feel caused by the missing Advantages and Benefits of your USPs. The intensity of the pain or gain desired is created by other methods used to establish the Buyer Beliefs "Need has Priority" and "ROI."

For example, you might ask, "What are your greatest areas of concern about _____?" "Where are the headaches?" "Where's the pain in this area?" "Where are your greatest concerns?" "How does _____ feel about that happening so often?" "Who's most frustrated about this?" "How does this affect _____?" "Who are the stakeholders?" "What would make that better?" "What are the costs involved?"

Prevent, Preempt, and Respond Strategies for Individual Objections

15. Objection: *Just send me your literature.*

> **When does it usually occur?** Initial contact.
> **Probable Cause:** Prospect does not feel any discomfort or see any gain.
> **Objective:** Increase awareness of the Benefit deficit discomfort or Benefit based gain.

Prevention Strategies:

1. Find the pain or find the gain. Getting the prospect's attention is the priority.
2. The quickest and easiest way to prevent this objection is to state during your opening remarks, that the reason you're calling is to get them some written information about how your company is solving some costly and critical issues related to three Unique Selling Points (USPs) related to prospect's job.
3. Given you have strong USPs; the prospect then will have the pain of unfilled needs because s/he does not have your USPs' Advantages and Benefits that fill these needs. If this is the right decision-maker to feel the pain or see the gain, s/he may not be able to do so because of distractions in other areas. For example, if you have a slight toothache and you plan to call the dentist when you get to work, but when you arrive, overwhelming customer demands occur that require your total attention. This takes all day. What happened to the toothache? That's right: the pain seemed less noticeable. Greater pain will distract you from milder

pain or discomfort. But when the day slows, the toothache pain returns to consciousness.

4. Get the prospect's attention by putting your greeting (good morning or good afternoon) at the end of your introduction, not at the beginning. For example, "Hello, this is ____ with ____, good morning." Wait until they respond. They may say something like, "I'm sorry, who did you say you're with?" That means you have their attention. Now you can answer, and then continue with the reason you are calling.

5. Introverts like to get printed materials before discussing substance. If you're calling on professions usually populated by Introverts (accountants, engineers, researchers, writers, actors, and so on) then you might add sending literature to your sales process steps. If you do this, be sure to tab the pages and use a highlighter to identify key items on the literature that you want them to be sure to notice, or you'll invite the "I haven't had time to look at it yet" type objection.

6. During pre-call planning, be sure the pain or gain you search for is in this person's area responsibility or authority (see decision-making roles).

Preemption Strategies:

1. "We have some options in this area. If now is a good time, let me ask you a couple of quick questions so that I can get you the right information."

2. "Before we go too much further, can I ask whether you have _____ (ask knockout qualifying questions)?"

Response Strategies:

1. "That's exactly what I want to do. And I want to save you time sorting through literature you don't need. With a couple of questions, I can narrow it down and tab the pages and highlight the information for you. Do you _____ or _____?"

2. "Good point; with the brochure, you can get more detailed information. Let me save you some time and tab the pages of the areas that you would be most interested in seeing. Would that be ___, ___, or ___?" From that answer, then ask the next set of questions related to their choice. For example, "What are your greatest concerns related to ___?"

3. "Great, what areas do you have your most serious concerns, ___, ___, or, ___?" Then, "Tell me what's going on there." Or "What would make that better for you?"

16. Objection: *Don't have time to discuss this now.*

> **When does it usually occur?** Early in the interaction.
> **Probable Cause:** Prospect does not feel any discomfort.
> **Objective:** Increase awareness of discomfort.

Prevention Strategies:

1. Find the pain or gain fast.
2. During your Approach/Positioning sales process step, the Benefit you give them during your opening remarks could be stated as relief of something negative. Use this strategy if this objection occurs frequently when you use the most positive approach. For example, "The

reason I'm calling is that I would like to get you some written information about how our company has solved some costly and critical issues related to ____, ____, and ____ (specify USP area). We found these to be responsible for lost revenues and increased corporate vulnerability in companies similar to yours."

2. Give them the "big bang" Benefit from the moment you speak to them. For example, "We now have ____ and ___ (USPs) that will ___ (Advantages and Benefits). If you've got just a moment, we can quickly discover which of these will work best for you. Do you want to do that now, or do you want to set a phone appointment for later today?" If later, then set the phone appointment.

Preemption Strategies:

1. If you've been warned, or if you know, from the type position the person is in, that this objection has a high probability, then one way to preempt it is to say right up front, "If you're like everyone else, I know you're pressed for time, so let me get right to it. The reason I'm calling is that I'd like to get you some written information about how our company has solved the costly issues related to ____ and ____ (USPs). To make sure I send just what you need, let me ask you a couple quick questions and we'll be done, fair enough?"

2. Getting permission to proceed is always a good idea. After using the above reason for calling script to make sure you've got their attention then ask, "Is this a good time, or would it work better for you if we set a telephone appointment for later today?"

Response Strategies:

1. "Okay, let's set another time, and just so I'm better prepared, what area concerns you most related to _____ (specify USP areas) the _____, the _____ or the _____?" Wait for a response then set a telephone appointment. "What is the best time for us to explore this area?"
2. "Thanks for letting me know. This is too important and there's too much at stake. When can we get just ten quick minutes to determine how much this is affecting your results? After that, we can set another time to go further into it."
3. Depending on how rushed the person sounds, choose number one above if they say they don't have time right now, but don't sound rushed. Choose number two if they indicate interest in getting the information but are in a rush.

17. Objection: *No one is paying attention to this area.*

When does it usually occur? After you introduce your products/services.
Probable Cause: Prospect does not feel any discomfort.
Objective: Increase awareness of discomfort or potential gain.

Prevention Strategies:

1. During your opening remarks, the "big bang" Benefit you give them could be stated as relief from something negative. For example, "The reason I am calling is that I would like to get you some written information about how our company has solved some costly and critical

issues related to ____, ____ and ____ (USPs)." Next, ask what this might be costing the prospect in actually budgeted dollars. For example, "We're seeing this add to about _____ ($ or %) in additional costs. Do you see yours as higher or lower?"

2. If you can quantify your "big bang" Benefit, then rattle it off from the start. No reason to hold back. For example, "We're working with three companies similar to yours and in the past three months, they've reduced their costs by 15%. From what I know about your operation, I think the opportunity for similar cost reduction is available, it's at least worth taking a couple of minutes to explore the possibility, isn't it?"

Preemption Strategies:

1. The prevention strategies above work very well to preempt this objection.
2. If what you sell isn't found on the company's list of strategic initiatives and it would be difficult to build a bridge, then you know you've got this objection in the making. One approach is to say it up front and then find the pain or gain. For example, "What we have here is not something that's usually on the priority list until people find out . . ." Now state your USPs.

Response Strategies:

1. "I'm sorry to hear that. I can understand how other things seem more urgent; in fact, many of my customers didn't pay much attention to this area until they found out just how much it was costing them. This is one of those hidden cost areas that really lights fires when people discover how much money is involved. To

make sure this isn't a major drain on your company, let me ask you just a couple of quick questions (don't pause) what are your greatest concerns related to _____ (USP)?"

2. "That's not unusual to hear because until now there really hasn't been an effective way to stop the losses. Let me ask a couple quick questions to see how fast this would impact your budget. How often are you seeing _____, _____, and _____ (Missing Advantages and Benefits of your USPs)?"

18. Objection: *We'll muddle through.*

When does it usually occur? After the initial introduction of your products/services.
Probable Cause: Prospect does not feel any discomfort.
Objective: Increase awareness of discomfort.

Prevention Strategies:

1. The "big bang" Benefit you give them could be stated as relief from something negative. For example, "The reason I am calling is that I would like to get you some written information about how our company has solved some costly and critical issues related to _____, _____ and _____ (USPs)." Follow this up by asking what this might be costing the prospect in real dollars in each of these areas. Be ready with your standards of legitimacy to keep this sale from stalling because the prospect doesn't know.

2. As with all these objections related to "no known need" or insufficient need, being quick on the uptake to create at least three gaps, and then quantify the costs

associated with them will prevent this objection most of the time.

Preemption Strategies:

1. Here, the Prevention Strategies work well to preempt a known objection.
2. Your strategy is to create solutions that are easy to use or are clearly a good trade-off from what they're doing now to what you could bring to the table. Use the "phrases of persuasion" (see answering the unanswerable objection) to pose the trade-off to the prospect. "That may be true. However, when you compare the two on ____, ____, and ____, I think you'll agree that this can become exceptionally more effective. Makes sense to take a few minutes to find out how much more effective, doesn't it?"

Response Strategies:

1. "That's certainly one way to do it. Another might be to calculate the costs associated with it to determine whether there might be a less expensive way to accomplish the same objectives. Some of our customers were not too pleased when they discovered the size of the hole this area created in their budgets. We can quickly get a gauge on this. As you think about _____ (USP area) what are your greatest concerns, what eats up your time or your staff's time?"
2. "I can certainly understand how you could feel that way. Many of my clients did too until they found out that they could get ____, ____, and ____ (USPs) for a fraction of the costs they were spending doing it the old

way. Maybe it's worth taking a couple minutes to see how much this would impact your daily budget?"

19. Objection: *It's too much hassle.*

When does it usually occur? When the prospect thinks about everything involved changing to your products/services.

Probable Cause: Prospect does not feel any discomfort.

Objective: Increase awareness of discomfort. The pain or gain must exceed the hassle of change.

Prevention Strategies:

1. During your Research Questions, identify the inefficiencies and hassle factors in the current methods of doing it.
2. Build up the hassle factor of continuing to do it the way they are currently meeting the need.
3. Build desire by highlighting the Benefit deficit (what they'll miss by not having the Advantages and Benefits of your Unique Selling Points).
4. Get them to fall in love with what you offer so much that they start building their own desire to get the Benefits and forget about the hassle involved. Or they love it so much that they see the larger hassle factor to their current methods. Think about a small sports car and the incredible hassle involved in getting in and out of it, servicing it, and the fact that it won't carry anyone but the driver and the mechanic. But oh do you look and feel good in it. Build the imagery for the prospect. Get them involved.

5. Take the fear out of the change process by detailing exactly what will change, how it will change, and how that will be implemented. Always balance each step in the change process with what won't change. Help the buyer imagine the change taking place and everyone, including the buyer, is not only safe but better off for making the change.

6. Review the Change Management Process section of this book for more ideas.

Preemption Strategies:

1. The "big bang" Benefit you give them could be stated as relief from something negative. For example, "The reason I am calling is that I would like to get you some written information about how our company has solved some costly and critical issues related to _____, _____ and _____ (USPs)." Ask what this might be costing the prospect in real dollars.

2. Structure your presentation about any change in how they currently do things to one or more of the four business needs (increase profits, decrease costs, enhance image, and minimize risks). Point out the hassle factor using their current process and how, once the change is made, that will be greatly reduced or disappear entirely.

3. "Let me stop and address one very big item, and that's the hassle factor involved in making any change. So one of the questions we'll want to answer is, 'Is it worth it?' And we can determine that very quickly. Let's start getting the answers by looking at ___, ___, and ___ (USPs)."

Response Strategies:

1. "That's a good point and I'm glad you brought that up. Hassle is not something we go looking for, and that's why we offer _____ because it does just that, removes the hassle. Let's compare the current process and what we're proposing to see whether our _____, _____, and _____ can significantly reduce the hassle factor of what you're doing now."

2. "I'm glad you brought that up. That's what many of my customers said too until they found out." Now explain away the hassle factor with your Unique Selling Points.

3. "Yeah, any change can be a hassle. However, when you compare the two processes (products) on their ability to _____, _____, and _____, I think the initial bit of hassle quickly fades once you start getting _____ ("big bang" Benefit). And to make that hassle seem less intrusive, we're offering to add some incentives to show our appreciation (name the incentives). That'll work, won't it?"

4. "Although it may seem like it's too much hassle, and it may seem to be easier to continue functioning the way you have been, don't you think it would be worthwhile to quickly calculate the costs associated with all the extra steps your team has to take, to determine whether there might be a less expensive and less frustrating way to accomplish the same objectives? When you think about _____ (area) what are your greatest concerns?"

20. Objection: *We won't use it.*

> **When does it usually occur?** After prospect discovers what you're selling.

Probable Cause: Prospect does not feel any discomfort to motivate change.
Objective: Increase awareness of discomfort.

Prevention Strategies:

1. During your pre-call planning phase, be sure the pain you search for is appropriate for this person's decision-maker role.
2. Use your Research Questions and Competitor Analysis information to find the pain or gain sooner than later.
3. Include in your opening remarks, "The reason I am calling is that I would like to get you some written information about how our company has solved some costly and critical issues related to ___, ___ and ___ (USPs)." If the costly and critical issues are in this person's decision-making role, then even if s/he doesn't think they'll use it, as a responsible person, s/he will still want to get the written information from a reputable company. Now you're passed this objection.
4. When you say costly and critical issues related to ____, state the Benefits the person could have but doesn't because s/he is not currently buying this product/service from you. It starts them thinking about the "discomfort" over the missing Benefits. If you're selling a pure commodity, then use USPs related to you and your company. See Differentiating Commodities section of this book.
5. Structure your presentation about usage to one of more of the four business needs: increase profits, decrease costs, enhance image, and reduce risks.
6. Connect your offering to one of the company's strategic initiatives championed by the chain of command.

Preemption Strategies:

1. "One of the major issues associated with any new way of doing something is getting people to embrace it and use it, so they can get the Benefits the company's paying to get. Knowing this, here's how we go about implementation." Now explain how you implement to ensure usage.
2. "Implementation is the next topic we should address. When your company purchases _____ (something categorically similar), how does it go about implementing in a way to ensure usage?"
3. See Stepped-Based Closing Strategies and the Change Management Process sections in this book to build a universal plan. Then you can say to the prospect, "A key component to making sure your usage rates will get the Benefits you want is to review our standard plan for implementation that incorporates the principles of change management. That way, even if in the end we don't move forward, you'll have an incredibly powerful plan to guide other changes you might need to make to your operation.

Response Strategies:

1. "That's an important point that I want to be sure to cover. What I'd like to do is put together a Plan for Implementation to make sure _____ is not only used by everyone involved but that they see how it clearly helps them in their job so they can enthusiastically embrace it. Let's start by looking at which staff will be using it."
2. "That's our next challenge. We have a template plan that incorporates the principles of change management

we can use to create a custom plan for implementation to ensure usage levels meet your expectations."

3. "I couldn't agree more. We've seen many implementations fall apart because two essential components are not done well. In fact, the industry standard is 50% fail. Our track record is 100% implementation by 90% of the staff and 80% implementation by 99% of the staff. So let's take a look at these two components. First and foremost, the participants must see and agree that it helps them do their job better, quicker, and easier. Second, they must see how it helps their customers, internal and external, get their needs met. So let's start here and see if these components are included in the plan, make sense?"

Chapter 19: Buyer Belief 5 – Need has Priority

Common Objections in this Category

21. No money budgeted, call me next year.
22. We're cutting back.
23. Not a priority now.
24. Timing's not right; see me next month/year.
25. I need to think this over.
26. Too many things in front of this.

Category Overview

An underlying factor causing this category of objections are the limited resources (money, time, talent) available when trying to satisfy all the competing needs in the company.

The first step to recalibrating priorities is to identify areas of discomfort and make certain that they're felt. The more concerns (pain from not having your USPs Advantages and Benefits) you can identify, and the more you can quantify subjectively, emotionally, and financially, the more they will feel a growing sense of urgency and the higher the priority becomes. The loudest "squeaky wheel" with the biggest ROI rapidly moves up in priority.

Discuss the Advantages and Benefits the prospect wants and quantify what not having them is costing each month out of their current budget. Show them where the money is in their budget.

Knowing where to look in their budget will emphasize the reality of the costs associated with this need. Unfortunately, this money is often located in ambiguous areas such as "higher than usual" operating costs. When this happens, you'll need the applicable industry standards of legitimacy to guide your discussions. You can often gather these standards by asking your customers for the guides they use.

Your ultimate goal is to move your products and services from the cost side of the budget to the revenue generating and profit enhancing side of the budget. When times get tough, this is where you'll want to be positioned.

Prevent, Preempt, and Respond Strategies for Individual Objections

21. Objection: *No money budgeted, call me next year.*

> **When does it occur?** When they find out what you're selling or when they hear the price.
> **Probable Cause:** Prospect recognizes the need exists and feels some discomfort, but has too many other priorities so there is no sense of urgency.
> **Objective:** Increase the priority of this need and create a sense of urgency.

Prevention Strategies:

1. Overall the strategy would be to increase priority by finding several smaller associated needs and by quantifying the financial, subjective, and emotional hidden costs of putting off these needs.

2. Profile Questions tell you the extent this prospect meets the critical characteristics of your most desirable customers and identifies their corporate values that will work as motivators.

3. Orient the topics of conversation to your Unique Selling Points (USP), and then determine through questions (FAB / TEA) the extent the prospect does not have their Advantages and Benefits.

4. Quantify what it is costing the prospect not to have the Advantages and Benefits of your USPs. Then, using these figures supplied by the prospect, show what it will cost over the next twelve months. Emphasize that this is real money in the current budget. Make sure you interview the managers of the departments whose budgets you impact. Present this information to the Final Authority (person over all the budgets you impact).

Preemption Strategies:

1. Tie meeting the USP generated needs to any known company-wide strategic initiatives. See the company's website and interview staff for this information.

2. Tie meeting the USP generated needs to a key manager's MBO.

3. Recognize that there may not be a budget item specifically labeled for funding this need. That means you'll have to find the money using other labels that compensate for not having a specific need met. For example, lack of insulation on a building could translate into higher heating and air-conditioning costs. If someone doesn't have the Advantages and Benefits of your Unique Selling Points, find out how and where they compensate to create a trade-off situation.

Response Strategies:

1. "Several of our customers, when they first looked into this, came to the same conclusion until we conducted a full cost-benefit analysis. What they found was that the money was there, but was hidden in several budgets under different headings such as, overtime, downtime, lost production, ___, ___, and ___. Let me propose we follow the same plan we used with them and conduct a cost-benefit analysis to easily cost justify the investment. Makes sense to take a few minutes to explore the possibility, doesn't it?"

2. After the cost-benefit analysis is completed or standards of legitimacy are given as interest generator, you could say, "As you can see, the current cost is ___ (point to or state amount). Over the next twelve months, you've allocated $ ___ in your current budget. The difference between what you are currently spending and what we recommend is $___. This means that for every month delay you lose $___ of your currently budgeted money. We can't compensate for what you've already lost, but what we can do is provide budget relief starting next month." Now, introduce your "Plan for Implementation" that includes your "Change Management Plan" as needed. Note that I intentionally tied "loss" to the current way of doing things and that I use the word "current" to emphasize that the money is there in the budget, regardless of how it's labeled.

22. Objection: *We're cutting back.*

When? Early in the process or at any time this "cutting back" event is announced.

Probable Cause: Prospect does not see what you offer as a profit generator. See cost factor but does not see the value to be in excess of what they are paying.

Objective: Move from the line-item cost side of the budget to the revenue-generating profit side of the budget. Make it clear how you will help lower their overall budget by using your products/services.

Prevention Strategies:

1. Position what you sell on the revenue-generating side of the budget.
2. Position what you sell on the cost-cutting side of the budget (lower bottom-line). For example, "Our product replaces these three products you're currently using and it removes the use costs in these areas helping you save almost __% from your current budget."
3. Review their corporate value system to provide you with guidance to help them set priorities in what to cut as it relates to your products/services.
4. Establish the use of your products/services as a means to reduce their overall costs. Focus on the bottom-line (total cost of ownership), rather than top line price.
5. Ask questions to discover who will have the most at stake so you can help them become your Champions.

Preemption Strategies:

1. Show them how to reduce their budgets by getting your products/services. Use their facts and figures when you do this. If that's not possible, use industry standards of legitimacy that they can agree on.
2. Since you already know this objection is lingering in the background, you might as well bring it up and

address it directly. For example, "It's that time of the fiscal year when companies start cutting back. So I want to make sure we can help you reduce your budget by replacing any high maintenance items with those that are maintenance free for the rest of the year."

Response Strategies:

1. "Several of our customers are in the same situation, and that means they not only have to look at what the price of the service is but also at what it costs them to use it. When they add those two, they can see the true bottom-line impact. So after we complete the cost-benefit analysis, I believe your ability to reduce the overall bottom-line by adding $10 to one budget, while at the same time saving $100 in another budget will make a better contribution to cost cutting. The question, as I see it, is do you focus on just one budget in cost cutting or all the budgets a particular product or service impacts, to structure the best ROI?"

2. "When you say 'cost cutting,' are you looking at just the price to get a product/service, or are you including the cost to use it, and any collateral costs associated with the company you choose to do business with?" So one of your criteria for selecting a supplier is that their impact on all affected budgets is lower than you are currently spending, and that will help you in your efforts to cut back?"

23. Objection: *Not a priority now.*

When does it usually occur? After the prospect hears your opening presentation.

Probable Cause: Prospect does not know the full cost related consequences of delaying action.
Objective: Quantify (financially and subjectively) what it will cost each month s/he delays.

Prevention Strategies:

1. Create a sense of urgency to own your product/service by identifying what it currently costs the prospect not to have your solution, then cast these costs into the future (for the next year, for example). Get the prospect to admit that these costs are somewhere in the budget.
2. Optionally, address several issues that have subjective, emotional and other qualitative costs to them. Get the prospect's agreement to those costs and the effects they have on staff, productivity, or quality.

Preemption Strategies:

1. Make a bold opening preemptive remark about the effects your product and service can have on the prospect. This will get their attention and help set up a yardstick style close to establish priority. For example, "I've studied your organization's processes in ____ (state area of expertise) and compared the key metrics to those in our customer base. Our current estimate is that we will be able to ____ (state result such as increase sales by a minimum of 26% in three months). Using the figures in your last annual report, 26% is $ ____. Getting those additional revenues would fall at what priority level in your organization?" One objective in doing this is to get the prospect to challenge you by asking you to prove your capability. When that happens, you now have implied permission to engage

them in a series of diagnostic questions designed to identify and confirm missing Advantages and Benefits provided by your Unique Selling Points (USPs). Next, quantify what it costs not to have these Advantages and Benefits using the prospects facts and figures. Finally, use irrefutable logic to point out that if they had the Feature that provides the missing Advantages and Benefits, then they wouldn't have the costs associated with not having them (or would have the improved revenue in this example).

2. From the beginning, bring up and connect the Advantages and Benefits of your proposed USP Features (capabilities) to one or more corporate initiatives. This automatically boosts its priority for review.

Response Strategies:

1. "Several of our customers came to the same conclusion until we conducted a full cost-benefit analysis. What they found was that the money was there, it was just in different budgets such as _____, _____ and _____ (USPs). So I propose we follow the same plan and conduct a cost-benefit analysis that will more than cost justify the investment and probably save the company money in the short run. Makes sense, doesn't it?"

2. "And that's exactly why I'm calling. This is not something that finds its way to the priority list except when it starts costing more in real dollars to ignore it than it does to go ahead and deal with it. Here's one quick example to see whether you're seeing these expenses continue to increase." Now using the missing USPs' Advantages and Benefits, point out how those

translate into real dollars and where, in their budget, this money shows up.

24. Objection: *Timing's not right; see me next month/year.*

> **When?** After the prospect becomes familiar with what you sell.
> **Probable Cause:** Prospect does not know the costs associated with delaying the decision.
> **Objective:** Quantify (financially and subjectively) what it costs each month s/he delays.

Prevention Strategies:

1. Quantify what it costs the prospect not to have the Advantages and Benefits of your Unique Selling Points (USPs).
2. Using figures supplied by the prospect, show what it will cost over the next twelve months.
3. Emphasize that this is real money in the current budget.
4. Ask whether this amount will go into next year's budget as well.
5. Make sure you have interviewed the managers of the departments whose budgets you impact. Present this information to the person in the Final Authority role.

Preemption Strategies:

1. Begin your preemption by connecting your Unique Selling Points' Benefits with the areas you impact. If you improve productivity, improve revenue generation or lower costs, then you want to state that up front. For example, if you could improve the profits on sales made by ten salespeople by 50% in 90 days, and you know

the customer's sales numbers (from whatever source), then it would be easy to introduce the amount of money you could help the customer capture. State it (as a range), and then say, "Let me show you how we do that." Now provide the logic of your claim, and then discuss how this could help the prospect.

2. Pinpoint the areas you can help the client (USPs) and state the logic of how it works as the basis for the discussion to follow. For example, "We use (Feature) solar energy connected to rechargeable batteries to power the lights. This means that (Advantage) you don't have to change and discard expensive batteries every month. From what I learned from maintenance, you have 1,000 locations that expend 24,000 batteries per month at an estimated cost of $15 per battery plus labor. Each system costs only $150. Do you have a few minutes to run the numbers on what this would mean in (Benefits) annual savings?" You can do this with any of your Unique Selling Points' FABs that are easily quantified.

Response Strategies:

1. "I will certainly do that and can I ask you a quick question? If your company spends budget dollars on _____ and _____ (state USPs cost savings areas), then that could add up to a fairly large amount at the end of the fiscal year. By the way, when does your fiscal year end? That could mean _____ months of extra payments, so perhaps it is worth taking a few moments to calculate to see if this project should shift in priority?"

2. "I know you want to make the change to a more efficient system, so isn't it true that taking the time now to quantify the results of this change is less important

than being able to plan and prepare for the improved results?"

25. Objection: *I need to think this over.*

When? After the presentation.
Probable Cause: Prospect does not believe the consequences of delaying response in this area are greater than other areas.
Objective: Quantify (financially, subjectively and emotionally) what it costs each month s/he delays.

Prevention Strategies:

1. Orient the conversation to your Unique Selling Points (USPs).
2. Quantify what it costs the prospect not to have the Advantages and Benefits of your USPs. Using the prospect's figures, show what it will cost over the next 12 months. Make sure to interview the managers of the departments whose budgets you impact.
3. For this to prevent the "think it over" objection your logic in how it comes together to produce results, must be thorough, irrefutable, and clearly understood by the prospect. Any uncertainties must be resolved.
4. Involve the prospect in generating a detailed list of the steps in the implementation process. Make sure all the "iffy" steps have backup plans. Incorporate the Change Management Process principles.
5. Ask the prospect "why" this plan will work. It's important to get them to defend the plan. See Creating Attitudes section in this book. The more they can defend each step, the more comfortable they will feel moving forward.

6. Ask the prospect how it will affect each key decision-maker for this project. It's important for them to anticipate positive responses from each key person. If there is a negative that just won't go away, then use what you're learning in this book to help them prevent, preempt, and respond to the objection or negative emotion (See Defusing Anger process).

7. This objection may also be the result several issues related to different "Buyer Beliefs" from sticker shock (ROI) to being overwhelmed by the volume of information (Best Solution), to wanting to explore options and suppliers (Capability & Credibility). And it is possible through various actions (yours and others) to cause Buyer Beliefs to become weak enough to stall the sales process. Finally, if you have a complex proposition, build in the "think it over" time and process as a part of your sales process.

Preemption Strategies:

1. You know you'll get this objection if you're working with a highly introverted person for whom you have not provided advance detailed written information about the project and what's expected of them. Build into your plan, a statement such as, "I think we've covered this thoroughly, but let's take a couple of days to really think this over. How much time do you think you'll want to do this?" Let the prospect reply then say, "Yes, that's about how much I'll need to review the plan as well. So let's get together again on ____." Take out your calendar (or mobile device) and set the appointment right then and there. Now send the meeting request so you'll get the response while you're still together.

2. Do you have a detailed list of all the steps necessary for someone to buy from you? See the various Step-Based Closing Strategies discussed earlier in this book. Tell the prospect that you want to be thorough and have a checklist of things critical to getting the project implemented. Now you can simply start asking questions about each critical step in the process. For example, "For the measurements, are there any other factors that could influence the fit?" "Do we need to spend any more energy on how the colors will blend?" "Are you comfortable with the process and safeguards we have to make sure you get the right colors?" Continue this process relevant to your product and service all the way to the money to be invested. At this point really explore the Return on Investment, Rate of Return, and Return on Assets as necessary. Make sure all the probable money questions are answered. Use your lists of Business Needs and Human Needs to guide your Benefit Questions.

Response Strategies:

1. "That makes sense. This is an important decision and you do need to feel comfortable with it. You want to make sure you've covered all of your bases. To help clarify my thinking, and perhaps to answer any questions you might have while I'm here, what is it that you wanted to think over (don't pause here). Is it (product/service) are you most concerned about, is it _____, or_____?" Now thoroughly review every FAB and step in the process. Again, as in the preemption strategy number two above, unless the prospect indicated that pricing is not an issue, deal with the money last.

2. "Good point. I know you want to make sure nothing slips through the cracks, and I'm right there with you. So wouldn't you prefer that we took that time together to do a review with my resources while I'm still here and available to answer any questions? That would be quicker than to try to find time to think all this through without those resources, especially for a project as time-sensitive as this one, wouldn't it?"

3. "And I think that's the next step for us. I want to go through each of these areas we've been discussing and review the plan to make sure the results we're targeting are the results we'll get. It won't take long to do this, but to do this right, I need your feedback, so, let's start with _____."

26. Objection: *Too many things in front of this.*

When? After you have presented your Benefits.

Probable Cause: Prospect does not believe the consequences of delaying the response in this area are greater than other areas.

Objective: Quantify and show the financial, subjective, and emotional costs each month s/he delays.

Prevention Strategies:

1. Orient the conversation to your Unique Selling Points (USPs). Quantify what it costs the prospect not to have the Advantages and Benefits of your USPs. Using the prospect's figures, show what it will cost over the next twelve months. Make sure to have interviewed the managers of the departments whose budgets you impact. Present this information to the Final Authority.

2. In a rapid-fire style, bring up three areas where the Benefits of your USPs prevent costs most likely to be found in the person's budget.

Preemption Strategies:

1. Recognize there are many holes in a ship that can sink it. Part of your prospect's job is to plug the largest and most costly holes first and keep the bilge pumps evacuating more water than is coming in. This is an understandable strategy. However, some smaller holes can be filled on the way to filling the bigger ones and some Benefits can increase the capacity of the bilge pumps. Position your Benefits as the type that plugs holes and increases capacity with the least effort made by the customer. What do you offer that decreases costs and increases revenues? Focus heavily on those areas.

2. As with many preemption strategies, it's best to state the objection diplomatically and then offer the best response. For example, "Many of my customers have a lot on their plates, and this project ordinarily doesn't get on their priority list until someone starts making noises about all the money being lost (or revenues lost). Especially since that could easily fix with a little effort on anybody's part. Just to be sure, let's do a quick cost-benefit analysis in a few key areas (USPs) to see whether the amount of money we're talking about is enough to trigger action. Let's focus first on ___ (USP), what would be a rough estimate of how often are you seeing ___ happen?" Wait for an answer. If not forthcoming, ask a conditional question such as, "If you did know, what would you guess it to be?" If s/he still doesn't know, then establish a standard of legitimacy to use until the actual numbers can be determined.

Continue now with what it costs each time it happens (or doesn't happen). Continue these strategies until you've covered your major Unique Selling Points (USPs) or you have enough money identified that could easily pay for your Features. Note that a "conditional question" removes the pressure of having to be right and is designed to give you an answer you can work with to continue the process.

Response Strategies:

1. "That's a good point. I'm glad you mentioned it. I can understand shifting priorities. Change is constant, isn't it? We have, however, been deciding priorities based on what it costs us each month not to solve the problem. If your company spends budget dollars on ____ and ____ (state USP cost savings areas), then that could add up to a fairly large amount at the end of the fiscal year. By the way, when does your fiscal year end? That could mean ____ months of extra payments that it is at least worth taking a few moments to calculate to see if this project should shift in priority, doesn't it?"

2. "And that's exactly why I'm here (why I'm calling). This is an inconspicuous area that can consume budget dollars and go almost undetected. Our track record shows that we can save companies as much as 65% on their bills, just by running them through our software. Let's take a couple of minutes to see how much money we're talking about. By the way, does your company offer a percentage of the savings to the person who discovers how to save it?"

Chapter 20: Buyer Belief 6 – Type Solution Will Work

Common Objections in this Category

27. *It just won't work for us.*
28. *We've never had good results with _____.*
29. *This isn't for us.*
30. *Don't want to stick our necks out on this.*
31. *You don't have what we need.*
32. *Your lead times are too long.*
33. *Management is taking a different track.*
34. *I need better quality than what you offer.*

Category Overview

You establish this Buyer Belief by demonstrating that without your Unique Selling Point's Feature, the prospect cannot possibly have its Advantages and Benefits. This is irrefutable logic ("if this, then that"). Always make the point with logic before you provide the backup data, references, and testimonials. Once the logic is in place, you can then use the Benefit Questions to trigger the necessary defense emotions, to create favorable attitudes, and to motivate purchase.

Prevent, Preempt, and Respond Strategies for Individual Objections

27. Objection: *It just won't work for us.*

When? After initial introduction commercial or after the full presentation.

Probable Cause: Prospect does not believe your type of solution will work.

Objective: Demonstrate and apply the irrefutable logic of your USP FABs.

Prevention Strategies:

1. The logical connection of the USP's Feature, Advantage and Benefit is irrefutable. For example, the container is made of plastic (F) so it won't rust (A), and that means fewer costly replacements (B) caused by rust.

2. Demonstrate your solution will work for them by connecting the problem to "not" having your USP Feature that provides the Advantages and Benefits that solve the problem. The logic is circular and irrefutable. Use the following steps to establish this logic (FAB / TEA):

    a. Orient to the topic of your USP Feature. Symptoms are the missing Advantages and Benefits. The problem is defined as the missing Feature (that provides the Advantages and Benefits).

    b. Quantify what it is costing the prospect not to have the Advantages and Benefits of your USP's Feature using the prospect's facts and figures.

    c. Use your Feature (or Feature category) to set a specification or criteria. Explain the Feature using its Advantages and Benefits. You could further explain how this will reduce the pain, solve the problem and eliminate the financial impact on the prospect's company. For example, "So one of your requirements for selecting another container is that it is made of a material that won't rust, so as you change over, you could start to reduce the costly part of the budget you have for replacing the rusting containers. Is that pretty much how you see it?"

Preemption Strategies:

1. If this objection comes at the end of your presentation, it may be related to the plan for implementation. The steps you've outlined might be too big for this person to take. They don't see how to get from step one to step two. In this case, you may need to simplify the steps and make them smaller and more logically sequenced with more safety valves for slowing or stopping the process. For example, you might say, "and after that step, if everything is still working for you, our next step would be to ____."

2. Tell a story about how your product/service worked for similar clients. Use words that create pictures. Several short stories are exceptionally effective in preempting this objection.

Response Strategies:

1. "It's difficult to see how this would work in this situation and that's because we haven't yet clarified whether you need it. One quick way to find out is to look at the ____ (orient to the category of your USP's Feature) and determine the levels of concern you have with ____, ____, and ____. Which of these areas give you the greatest concerns?"

2. "I am not sure I fully understand. What experiences have you had with this type of product/service?" Use your Active Listening Skills to establish your right to be heard. Set as a condition or specification, what you can do, that will counter the previous experience, and then return to orientation in each area the prospect brought up. For example, "It was a good product/service but we couldn't get anyone to use it." You might respond with, "Yes, we've seen that before. So one of your requirements to even consider this type of product (or service), is that a plan would be developed to ensure that it will be used as designed, so the company can get the Benefits they're paying for?" With an affirmative response, orient to the planning process. Your goal is to do planning at the end of each session including writing action items resulting in a detailed plan of implementation before piloting the project. See Step-Based Closing Strategies section of this book.

28. Objection: *Never had good results with _____.*

When? When product/service is first mentioned.
Probable Cause: Prospect does not believe your type of solution will work.
Objective: Demonstrate and apply the irrefutable logic of your USP FABs.

Prevention Strategies:

1. Demonstrate your solution has capabilities that will make it work for them by using the following steps (FAB / TEA):

a. Orient to the topic of your USP's Feature. Symptoms are the missing Advantages and Benefits. The problem can, therefore, be defined as the missing Feature that provides the Advantages and Benefits.

b. Quantify what it is costing the prospect not to have the Advantages and Benefits of your USPs.

c. The specification to set is the USP's Feature, (or the Feature's category). Explain the Feature using its Advantages and Benefits. Talk about how this will reduce the pain, solve the problem and eliminate the financial impact on the prospect's company. Make sure the FABs are logical ("if this, then that").

2. Note that if this objection comes at the end of your presentation it may be related to the plan of action for implementation. In this case, you may need to simplify the steps, make them smaller, and include more steps that provide feedback.

Preemption Strategies:

1. If you've been alerted to this objection or if it's one you commonly hear, then you'll want to start your introduction with a comparison between what they might have experienced and what you're offering. For example, asking the prospect whether they've seen the "night and day difference" between version one and version two. If the problem is related to weight, size, color, density or whatever, create an analogy that dramatically shows the difference between what they experienced and what you're offering.

2. During your opening remarks, you might point out that the results of the earlier versions of this type of product or service were mixed at best. However, with steadfast

advancements made in your industry, successful implementation, and results are now the norm that companies routinely experience. Now tell a one or two brief success stories. Include early attempts that failed but that now led to success.

Response Strategies:

1. "What did you try before? What were you using before that? You decided to improve how you were doing ___ and it didn't work out the way you had anticipated. I still think it was a good decision because the Benefits are definitely there. Things have changed so rapidly in this area to improve implementation and usability, that perhaps we should explore this a little further. Tell me about . . ."

2. "I am not sure I fully understand the experiences you've had with this type of product/service. What happened?" Use your Active Listening Skills to establish your right to be heard, and then focus on what you can do that will counter the previous experiences. Next, return to each area the prospect brought up. For example, "It was a good product/service but we couldn't get anyone to use it." You might respond with, "Yes, we've seen that before, and so one of your requirements to even consider this type of product/service again, is that a workable plan would be developed to ensure that the product/service is used to its optimal levels, so the company can get the Benefits they're paying for?" With an affirmative response, orient to the planning process then lock in planning at the end of each session and write the action items to develop a detailed plan of implementation before piloting the project. See Step-Based Closing Strategies in this book.

29. Objection: *This isn't for us.*

> **When?** After initial introduction commercial or after the full presentation.
> **Probable Cause:** Prospect does not believe your type of solution will work.
> **Objective:** Demonstrate and apply the irrefutable logic of your USP FABs.

Prevention Strategies:

1. Use your USPs to guide your Research Questions to find prospect's needs.
2. When talking with the prospect, focus in areas where you are strong, the competitor is weak and the prospect has needs. Demonstrate how your solution will work for them by using the logic of how the Feature has Advantages in how it provides Benefits that fill needs to solve problems. Use the missing Advantages and Benefits to identify the need for the Feature (FAB / TEA).
3. Quantify what it is costing the prospect not to have the Advantages and Benefits of your USP. Use the irrefutable logic described above. Ask the prospect about the extent they would expect to get the Benefits. Asking puts the burden of proof on them as the person making the claims is responsible for proving them.

Preemption Strategies:

1. Tell a story about customers who initially didn't think this would be for them but with the USPs you offer, they were able to benefit immensely. Now here's the key, after the story, ask the prospect to speculate about

the Benefits the customer in the story got and how they could apply to what your prospect would like to get. Ask what Benefits would be important or even critical for them to receive so they would feel comfortable owning your product/service.

2. Start your conversation by saying, "This isn't for everyone. This is for people who ____." Now describe the characteristics of the person (company) who Benefits the most from your product and service. If the person you are talking with will not benefit, then ask for referrals. Note that when listing the characteristics you're looking for in a prospect; define as narrowly as possible. This will reduce the number of potential prospects to a manageable number for your referral source to handle.

Response Strategies:

1. "Although it may seem that this isn't something for you, let's conduct a cost-benefit analysis that will determine whether our solution will help you with ___ (prospect's problem). Sound good?"

2. "And that's why I want to be absolutely sure this isn't right for you, because if it is, you stand to get a significant cost reduction to how you ___. Sometimes it's not obvious so just a few quick questions and we'll both know for sure. That makes sense doesn't it?" Next orient to your USPs, ask your qualifying questions, ask your USP guided Research Questions, and start discovering the prospects' greatest concerns about "not having" the Benefits they offer.

30. Objection: *Don't want to stick our necks out on this.*

When? After initial introduction commercial or after the full presentation.
Probable Cause: Prospect does not believe your type of solution will work.
Objective: Demonstrate and apply the irrefutable logic of your USP FABs.

Prevention Strategies:

1. Demonstrate how your solution will work for them. Uncertainty about getting the expected Benefits causes this anxiety based objection.
2. The logic of how your Feature delivers specific Advantages and Benefits that fill the identified need must be solid.
3. Continually ask the prospect to explain how getting the Advantages and Benefit would logically flow from having the Feature that provides them. The more they can define this, the stronger the link will become. Use your Benefit Questions extensively. The person making the claim assumes the burden of proof.
4. Use a standard plan for implementation that has worked successfully in the past for other customers of this size and industry. Tell brief stories about critical steps to provide clear examples of how they are implemented.
5. Make sure the plan for implementation is simple, small steps, clear milestones with bailout clauses. Include informational progress reports at regular intervals and at all milestones. Incorporate Change Management principles into your lists. See Change Management and Step-Based Closing Strategies sections of this book.

Preemption Strategies:

1. The first step in getting past the anxiety is to help the prospect see that doing nothing might put Benefits they currently enjoy at risk. This sets the stage to get them to admit that they will have to do something. If not this, then what? Now you know who or what you'll be competing with and can conduct the standard sales structured Competitor Analysis.
2. Walk them through each step of the process continually asking how that would work in their situation. Ask about options to make it even better. Fully engage their imagination. For example, if you have a tangible product, you might ask them where they would put it. Once they can visualize it in place, you've overcome a huge barrier. If you have an intangible service, then ask feeling (emotion) type questions to help make it more tangible to the prospect. For example, "How would that feel, knowing you've got that covered?" Or "How do you think people feel when they have access to this?"

Response Strategies:

1. "I understand how you feel, in fact, many of my customers felt that way too, until they found out that they really needed to resolve this issue. So they took the route of doing it with the smallest amount of risk possible. What seems to make sense at this point is for us to review how the Benefits we're offering would indeed solve the problem. Then once you're satisfied we've got the solution and if the cost-benefit analysis works, we can then look at the plan for implementation that we've used successfully many times before. But, even as confident as we are, let's identify the steps you

would feel more comfortable with if you have backup plans. How does that sound so far?"

2. "That's a good point. We don't want the risk to outweigh the Benefits and as we see it, taking any action, without a clearly defined plan for implementation, is risky. What I'd like to discuss is the standard plan for implementation that we have used successfully in the past with companies similar to yours. As we go through the steps, milestones, progress reporting, and measurements, we'll customize it for you. So here is the basic plan. Let's start with step number one and make adjustments as we work our way through the list."

3. "I know you're concerned about the risk involved with this strategy, but wouldn't you prefer to have this settled once and for all? It's at least worth taking a close look at how we can minimize the risk, isn't it?"

4. "While eliminating all risk seems vital at the moment, in the long run, your ability to get this project up and running dominates your decision, doesn't it? (Don't pause), So, to be sure, let's look at each step and contingency plans we have in place, and then we'll be in a better place to make a choice on whether to move forward, make sense?"

31. Objection: *You don't have what we need.*

When? After initial introduction commercial or after the full presentation.

Probable Cause: Prospect does not believe your type of solution will work.

Objective: Demonstrate and apply the irrefutable logic of your USP FABs.

Prevention Strategies:

1. Match this prospect with the profile characteristics of your most desirable current customers to make sure they are qualified.
2. Conduct research to determine how your products and services would fit within the prospect's work-flow process. Use your USPs guide you in this research to find the prospect's needs.
3. Orient the topic of conversation in the areas where you are strong, your competitor is weak, and the prospect has needs.
4. Once you have the recognition that a problem exists, quantify what it costs the prospect not to solve it, and then set your Unique Selling Point's Feature as the criteria for selecting a solution (FAB / TEA). When this is done, the prospect will, in effect, rule out the current supplier because they can no longer meet the requirements or specifications.
5. Note that if this objection comes at the end of your presentation it may be related to the plan of action for implementation. In this case, you may need to simplify the steps, make them smaller, and include more steps to provide feedback. See Change Management and Step-Based Closing Strategies sections of this book.

Preemption Strategies:

1. "We're coming to you today with an approach that at first glance may not seem to fit, but let me assure you right now, it does. We've studied your work processes, and while this is a novel idea, it does work. We think it will work better than most traditional approaches. Thomas Edison said, 'Make it a point to keep on the

lookout for novel and interesting ideas that others have used successfully. Your idea has to be original only in its adaptation to the problem you are currently working on.' So let's take a quick look at what we're proposing so we can all review it in light of the extent you think it will achieve the results you want. Does this make sense?"

2. "Our company has been adding new products to better meet the needs of our customers. We can now meet your requirements and exceed your expectations in this area. Here's an idea to consider when looking at improved ways to meet your needs for ____ (specify). What's really special about this is ____, and that means ___. How do you see this reducing the cost of ___ (state a relevant business need)?" Tell the Feature of your USP, explain it with the Advantages and ask about how the Benefit will meet their needs (FAB / TEA). For example, "The containers we can now provide are made of plastic (F) so they won't rust (A). How do you see this helping to reduce your rusted barrel replacement budget (B)?"

Response Strategies:

1. "Based on your application, that's the same conclusion I was about to make. Then, as I was reviewing your workflow process in this area, I remembered another customer and how we discovered ____ (state area strength to corresponding competitor weakness) was really running up some hidden costs. I'd like to explore what these costs might be for your company to see if it's worth it to you to fix it. That makes sense doesn't it?"

2. "It's certainly possible that I misunderstood your needs. Tell me how you're defining what your needs are in this area?" Now use Active Listening. After they described what they need, you can continue with, "So let me review how I'm interpreting these needs, okay?" Wait for agreement, then start with the basics and orient to the areas you have USPs. If there are areas you can meet the overall needs, but perhaps not one or two of the smaller needs such as color, then use one of the objection trade-off phrases of persuasion. For example, "That may be true, however, let's compare the two on ____, ____, and ____ (USPs) and I think you'll agree that the trade-off we have here more than compensates for that, don't you?"

32. Objection: *Your lead times are too long.*

When? After prospect learns your lead times for product/service delivery.

Probable Cause: Prospect does not believe that your type of solution will work.

Objective: Clarify with "irrefutable logic" how the Advantages and Benefits of your product outweigh the extra lead time.

Prevention Strategies:

1. Focus the conversation with the prospect in areas you are strong, your competitor is weak and the prospect has needs. This will assure that the solution to the problem will include your USPs.
2. Set your USPs as criteria for selection, this will help the prospective customer rule out your competitors and assure that your solution is the best option. This is a

critical component. The more USPs you can set as minimum specifications or requirements, the more the prospect will be limited in the choices they can make to select a supplier.

Preemption Strategies:

1. Lead times that exceed the prospect's expectations can be a deal-breaker for sure. So it's important to know whether the customer is talking about an estimated or target date, a due date, or a drop-dead date (not here by this time the order is automatically canceled so don't bother shipping because we won't accept it). If your lead times are long, then you should spend some time exploring the customer's needs in this area.

2. Backup plans should be included in your "plan for implementation" just in case your lead times get inadvertently stretched to the point of hurting your customer.

3. You may want to explore substitutions during the wait time.

Response Strategies:

1. "Although our lead times may seem long, isn't it worth waiting for a solution that will provide the long-term Benefits you really need? What will you base your decision on, the long-term Benefits our product/service will provide or getting a product/service in a shorter time but that will not provide you with the same Benefits?"

2. "Sure, you can get something quicker. But is that what you really want? Based on our conversation, I don't see how you could be happy with something less than we

talked about. Before you make a final decision, what do you say about taking a look at what you could use temporarily while yours is being built?"

33. Objection: *Management is taking a different track.*

When? Presenting what you sell.

Probable Cause: Prospect does not believe your type of solution will work better than management's track.

Objective: Establish, using "irrefutable logic" that the Advantages and Benefits of your solution will work best in solving the problem. Meeting with the right decision-makers may be a step we missed but now will need to be corrected.

Prevention Strategies:

1. During the research phase of the sales process, discover the prospect's business plans related to your products/services. This will point to management's direction in your product/service area. You can find much of this type of information on the prospect's website, in their annual reports, and in their brochures.

2. Identify any strategic initiatives that your product or service will help them achieve.

3. Meeting with the right decision-makers is critical in any sale. Confirm the types of decisions the person you're meeting with would make (ROI, Specifications, and so on). Ask this decision-maker to be your coach or sponsor to help you identify and set up meetings with the other decision-makers.

Preemption Strategies:

1. As a general practice, identify the characteristics of companies where top-down decisions are common. This could include companies with new leadership, in a volatile market, undergoing a change in size (up-or-down), undergoing a change in products/services, in an acquisition mode (all nonessential funding stops), and other characteristics.

2. Align your Customer Value Proposition (CVP) with whatever direction management decides to take. Show how what you offer will support and be important to achieving this new objective.

3. Change generates anxiety. Become the comforting common ground product/service that management and others affected, know and trust.

4. Find where you fit into the new direction and reposition yourself there.

5. For many companies, their development process includes a "make or buy" decision point. If you sell a product or service that fits into this situation, then you need to know where they are in this process to know how to proceed.

Response Strategies:

1. "I'm glad to see that management feels this is an important enough area to invest the time and resources necessary to devise a solution. In fact, we have worked with several management teams who started in this direction until they found out that when they compared their solution with what we already have available, especially in the areas of ____, ____, and ____ (USPs) they felt that the hidden costs needed to compensate for

these areas were more than they had budgeted. You may be at that point. It's probably worth taking a few moments to explore the possibility, isn't it?"

2. "This is not the first time we've been a part of this type of shift in direction. And if our experience is correct, then our product/service could be vital to the long-term success of that newly defined strategic direction. Just to be sure, tell me more about the direction management is taking."

34. Objection: *I need better quality than what you're offering.*

When? After initial introduction commercial or after the full presentation.

Probable Cause: Prospect does not believe your level of quality (type of solution) is sufficient.

Objective: Use irrefutable logic to demonstrate and establish that your type of solution offers the level of quality required for the job.

Prevention Strategies:

1. Recognize that it's not uncommon for some customers to want a level of quality way beyond what they need to get the job done. This is like buying fine china to take on a picnic where paper plates would work better.

2. Compare the qualifying characteristics of this prospect with your most desirable customers for the level of quality you offer.

3. Conduct research to determine how your products/services would fit within the prospect's workflow process to help them make money, lower costs, strength image or lower risks. Let your USPs guide you to finding the prospect's business needs.

4. Work with the prospect to determine the level of quality needed to be successful.

Preemption Strategies:

1. Determine quality standards. Reset them using the FAB / TEA strategy as needed to ensure the customer's needs are met.
2. List the specifications needed to do the job then move to the lowest common level (meets minimum specifications) that would include the greatest number of options. This would include most levels of quality needed to do the job, including yours. Review Multi-Bid Summary Form section in this book for ideas.
3. Now that your quality level is acceptable, shift to setting your USPs as part of the specification package. Orient the customer to your USPs, ask about the missing Advantages and Benefits and how they impact the customer getting their needs met.
4. Quantify what it costs them (financially, subjectively, and emotionally) not to have your USP's Advantages and Benefits (FAB / TEA).

Response Strategies:

1. "That's a good point and I'm glad you brought it up. It is true that the quality level of your current products/services is higher than what we provide. However, the real question is deciding the appropriate level of quality that will provide you with the highest rate of return, and still reliably perform to standard?" Pause, and then continue with, "This is like asking if you need to take fine china or paper plates on a picnic. So while it may seem vital at the moment to get and pay

for the highest quality available, in the long run, your ability to get the appropriate level of quality that will reliably do the job, will weigh heavily on your decision, won't it?"

2. "When I first evaluated the quality level we offer, I came to the same conclusion, but then, my manager pointed out that our customers are going on picnics and need paper plates, not fine china. So spending a lot of time and money to take it to the next level would put us in the premium category and that would be reflected in the higher price you'd pay and not in the functional effectiveness of the product/service."

Chapter 21: Buyer Belief 7 – Capability and Credibility

Common Objections in this Category

35. We want someone in our industry.

36. How do you know it will do that?

37. Never heard of you.

38. You're not large enough to handle the job.

39. I don't like your company.

40. I don't like your products/services.

41a. You don't understand our problems (Needs not uncovered).

41b. You don't understand our problems (Trust issue).

41c. You don't understand our problems (Company credibility issue).

42. Your track record isn't strong enough.

43. We had a bad experience with your company.

44. That can't be done.

45. I don't believe it.

46. I've never heard of your company.

47. You'll have to prove that to me.

48. We've never had good results with _____.

49. Your _____ is not good enough.

50. We only buy name brands.

51. You don't have what we need.

Category Overview

Without some level of credibility and trust, people just won't buy no matter what the opportunity or price. Your company's credibility will help establish trust in you and trust in you will help establish your company's credibility.

Capability and Credibility: Capability means you can to do what you say you can do. Credibility means believability. You do what you say you will do.

Trust and Rapport: Trust means belief without proof. Rapport means to be in harmony with the other person or group in manners, behavior, attitudes, dress, speech, values, and other ways. Harmony means that we are very much alike in certain ways. The more you are like me; the more I believe I can predict how you will act in certain situations. Therefore, I can trust you to behave as I would behave in these situations.

Standard methods to build Capability and Credibility: Website, Corporate Brochures, Testimonials, Client List, Referrals to Key Decision-Makers, Linking Benefits to Strategic Initiatives.

Standard methods to establish Trust and Rapport: Pacing and Leading, Common Ground, Personal Credentials, Active Listening Skills, Asking USP Guided Research Questions, Building Coaches, Mentors, and Champions, and using the FAB / TEA formula.

See Chapter 4: Capability and Credibility for more information.

Prevent, Preempt, and Respond Strategies for Individual Objections

35. Objection: *We want someone in our industry.*

> **When?** Initial contact or presentation.
> **Probable Cause:** Prospect does not believe you have the capability or credibility in their specific industry.
> **Objective:** Build capability and credibility.

Prevention Strategies:

1. Use referrals to gain entry to a new market.
2. Implement selected methods to build capability & credibility and to establish trust & rapport.
3. Send the Thomas Edison quote: "Make it a point to keep on the lookout for novel and interesting ideas that others have used successfully. Your idea has to be original only in its adaptation to the problem you are currently working on."
4. If their mission statement has any comments related to innovation, be sure to include this information in your presentation.
5. Emphasize the need to see and agree on the logic of the solution before determining who will implement. If it doesn't make sense logically, it won't get the support no matter who implements it.

Preemption Strategies:

1. Start with the standard methods to build capability & credibility and to establish trust & rapport. When you

select one or more of these methods, always note how you know that it's been done.

2. In your opening remarks, name three or four companies and their industries where you've had success. Next, identify and tell the three or four characteristics they had in common that contributed to the success. Finally, identify those same characteristics in their industry and more specifically, their company. Tell the prospect you expect to achieve success by blending your product expertise with their industry expertise and because the payoff could be exceptional, you'd like the opportunity to explore that possibility. When they agree, they will provide you with the necessary industry knowledge along the way so you can draw on your experience.

3. Start with the Edison quote, put it in your e-mail signature line; add it to your proposals, and any other custom written materials when you're prospecting in a new target market.

Response Strategies:

1. "I can certainly understand wanting someone in the industry to handle this project. Unfortunately, there are few people (companies, products, and so on) available. What we can do is interview your staff involved in the project to learn how we need to adapt our ____ (materials, equipment, service strategy, and so on) so the final solution can be as seamless as possible. The biggest Benefit from using this strategy is that we can truly bring an unbiased opinion. So while it may seem vital to have someone with this specific industry experience, in the long run, your ability to get the job done seamlessly is what's going to dominate your decision isn't it?"

2. "That's a good point and I'm glad you brought it up. We are not experts in your industry. Our expertise is in solving this type problem and then adapting the solution to your particular situation. The solutions team will have people on it from your company to provide the necessary industry guidance. So what will you base your decision on, getting someone with experience in the industry with little experience with this problem or getting someone with expertise with this type of problem, where you can provide industry and company guidance?"

3. "That's the first thing that came to my mind, then I found out, that when you look around your office at all the things you use, you have to ask yourself how many were invented just for this industry, and then, how many used components common to several industries? So while it is essential to have someone on the team with strong industry experience to provide the necessary guidance, in the long run, your ability to get a solution that will work is what will dominate your decision, isn't it?"

36. Objection: *How do you know it will do that?*

When? During or after the presentation.
Probable Cause: Prospect does not believe you have the capability or credibility in their specific industry.
Objective: Build capability and credibility.

Prevention Strategies:

1. The person making the claims must defend them. By first setting up irrefutable logic with the FAB / TEA formula, the burden of proof moves from you to them.

For example, "The containers are made from UV resistant plastic so they won't rust and won't deteriorate in the sun. How do you see this affecting your replacement budget for rusting containers?"

2. Emphasize the need to see and agree on the logic of the solution before looking for references or research studies.

3. Ask the prospect about select Benefits they will receive from having their needs met. Tie these types of questions to your USP Features and Advantages that deliver the Benefits you're asking about.

4. Use corporate marketing product brochures that demonstrate, explain and provide references for some function the prospect needs to be performed for support.

5. Create a foundation for each stage of the project with testimonial letters and references. Don't rely on them to make the sale for you. Use them only to support issues related to doing something different and having a system in place to ensure that it worked for the client.

Preemption Strategies:

1. Tell a story about a customer in a similar situation to the one your prospect finds him or herself in today. Your story will tell how, by using your products and services, your customer solved their problem. Unusual results, beyond ordinary capabilities, if not over emphasized, will have a positive effect. The story will gain strength if you have a testimonial letter stating the situation, or if you can put this prospect in touch with your customer.

2. Higher or Alternate Authority closing strategies work well here. Simply bring in someone else who can

substantiate your claim as a routine part of your interaction at this stage in your sales process. The alternate authority could be any credible person inside or outside the prospect's company. Sometimes they can even be from inside your company.

3. Include beta tests and pilot studies as a part of the implementation.

Response Strategies:

1. "We know it will do that because what we are talking about is based on the logic that you and I developed. First, we discovered that the cause of the concerns you have and the costs you are incurring are because you don't have a way to _____ (USP's Advantages and Benefits). That gives us some very strong logic to support this plan. In the long run, your ability to have ironclad logic will dominate the decision no matter how many people in other companies say it works for them. Your company is different, so the logic takes precedence, doesn't it?"

2. "At this time, the only thing you and I have is some very solid logic on which to base the decision. Your circumstances are different than those in other companies so we have to go with the logic. If the logic isn't solid then it doesn't matter how many people say it works in their companies, we must first be convinced of the logic. Once we've done that, then our Beta tests and Pilot studies will confirm that we're on the right track for your company, make sense?"

37. Objection: *Never heard of you* (personal)

> **When?** Initial Contact.
> **Probable Cause:** Prospect has little or no information about your capabilities or credibility. The customer may know about your company, just not you.
> **Objective:** Build trust and rapport and company capability and credibility.

Prevention Strategies:

1. For larger accounts, send a letter of introduction. Make it formal and first class. Let the prospect or customer know you will be calling them to set up a meeting. Have a call objective in mind. For example, having a new product that solves a known problem for this customer. Just "stopping by to meet you" is too weak and would probably get rejected by busy managers and executives.

2. If you're replacing someone in your company, ask them to make a call to introduce you or leave a message citing your credentials.

3. Decision-makers want to know whether you can get a resolution to issues and answers inside your company. Do you have the inside connections to get things done for the customer? If so, add how and why you can do that to your credentials.

4. Ask a manager to send an e-mail introducing you and citing your credentials. Include in the message that you'll be contacting them to (state call objective).

Preemption Strategies:

1. Write at least two elevator speeches. The first one contains one or two bold statements about your "big bang" benefits that will capture the prospect's attention in ten seconds or less. The second can be a half-minute to a minute long telling more about who you are, what you do, who you do it for, and how you're better (USPs) to explain the stellar results you get (and perhaps highlighted in your ten-second speech). Once done, ask for permission to continue to engage or re-engage. For example, "Can I send you a link to the information?" Or "Did I catch you at a good time to quickly verify some information?" Or you can show how on-target you are by moving forward asking USP guided Research Questions before engaging the FAB / TEA formula. The secret to an effective elevator speech is to practice, rewrite, practice, rewrite and practice again until you get the results you want.

2. Position yourself so the customer sees an immediate Benefit in working with you. One sales trainer gained instant credibility, not because he had any sales experience at all, but rather because he studied successful and unsuccessful salespeople. He said he was there to share what he discovered. For example, he said he would teach them the five skills the top performing salespeople used to make sale after sale, and he would share how the worst had three hidden traits that caused them to lose sale after sale. That kept the salespeople in his audience attentive to his every word. Now back to you. What makes you different? What special or unusual characteristics, skills, or knowledge do you bring to the table? How can you

position and communicate that to get and keep your prospects' attention?

Response Strategies:

1. "And that's exactly why I'm contacting you. My background with ____ will enable me to provide ____ for you, make sense?"
2. "That's true. However, when you consider the expertise I can bring to your organization as a _____ (state special credentials) and the volume of ____ you're using, I think you can see how we might capitalize on my experience to increase production while lowering your overall costs. Let's set a meeting to explore how to make this work. I have time available ___, ___, or ___. Which of those would work best for you?"

38. Objection: *You're not large enough to handle the job.*

When? After the presentation of the company's general information.
Probable Cause: Prospect does not believe you have the capability for the job.
Objective: Build capability and credibility.

Prevention Strategies:

1. Determine size potential based on matching profile characteristics of your most desirable customers and this prospect. If size potential is larger than normal, make plans with management about how they can increase capacity.
2. During your introductory remarks, include a description of how your company adjusts capacity based on the size

of the order. Present this information in a "matter of fact" or "routine" manner.

Preemption Strategies:

1. Level the playing field by bringing up the fact that in any large-scale project, it's the HR function with the processes to select the right skills, and it's the Project Managers who guide the application of those skills that can make-or-break any project, no matter what the size. Then point out what your organization does to ensure those functions are given consistent priority.
2. Talk about the ability to "scale" for different projects using the prospect's own subcontractors and consultants they feel would be competent for the job.

Response Strategies:

1. "I can understand your concern in that area; in fact, some of our larger customers said pretty much the same thing, until they found out . . ." Explain how you served large customers in the past.
2. "That's a valid concern using the standard method of handling everything by one supplier. In today's economy, most of us don't have that range of talent on board as employees, but what we all do is maintain access to this talent pool through independent contractors. That's how we get top talent at a reasonable investment. That makes sense, doesn't it?"

39. Objection: *I don't like your company.*

When? Initial contact.

Probable Cause: Prospect's dissatisfaction is caused by some reputation issues or as a direct result of neglect, uncaring interactions, poor business practices, public-relations issues, or philosophical differences. This can also occur when unrealistic expectations are set.

Objective: Reestablish credibility with realistic expectations.

Prevention Strategies:

1. Often the only consistent way to prevent this type objection is through continual public-relations efforts, creating a great place for employees to work, exceptional training, staff involvement in the community, and corporate outreach.

2. If the prospect buys your type product, is familiar with your company, yet buys from a company that uses a significantly different approach to conducting business, then this issue will be present, spoken or not. To prevent this, you need to understand the differences in how they do business from how your company does business, and why customers prefer their business model. You do this with your Competitor Analysis. If you need to make changes internal to your company, propose those to management.

3. For your prospect, first, establish similarities between your company and the competitor's, and then neutralize the competitor's strengths by discussing and getting agreement on how your processes are just as good as the competitor's. Next, shift the conversation to where

you are strong, the competitor is weak and the prospect has needs. Use your USPs to guide your Research Questions, and then use the FAB / TEA formula to lock in the logic and trigger attitude creating emotions.

Preemption Strategies:

1. Establish realistic expectations. For example, "We've had some difficult growing pains in our company that we recognize has led to some customer dissatisfaction. Fortunately, our management does have its heart in the right place and has taken action to fix these things. What I'd like to do today is talk with you about the specific areas where you've encountered challenges with our company. Tell me what happened." Use your Active Listening Skills like you've never used them before. Especially use the Reflect Emotion skill. Don't add to the content or become defensive in any way. Don't try to provide excuses or even answers at this time. Be thorough and find the rough spots that caused the issues. Then use the three steps to defuse negative emotions.

2. When you recognize any negative emotion from any person you're talking with, directed at you or not, follow the Defusing Anger process (Recognize, Apologize, and Solutionize).

Response Strategies:

1. "I'm sorry to hear that, could you tell me how that happened?" Use your Active Listening Skills and be sure to reflect any emotion and defuse any anger. "Based on what you've seen/heard I can understand how you came to that conclusion, in fact, I'd probably

make the same one. Like most companies, we've come a long hard way since then. In a sense, we're trying to become extremely good at ____, just to outweigh what we couldn't do in the past. And that's why I'm talking with you today. If you were to look at your ____ (workflow process) in the areas of ___, ____, and ___ (USPs) which of these are your greatest areas of concern?"

2. "And that's exactly why I'm calling. We've made some significant changes to our organization and the processes we use as a direct result of the feedback we've gotten from our customers. My job is to make sure the areas that caused you to dislike us are clarified and dealt with effectively. To do this, would you mind reviewing the circumstances for me?" Your immediate objective is to get them to start talking with you so you can continue to defuse their negative emotions using the technique outlined in the preemption strategy above.

3. First, actively listen to make sure the prospect knows that you understand their experience. Defuse any negative emotions, and then say, "Yeah, that was an eye-opener for our company and now we've come a long way since then. Like many companies, we instituted a Total Quality Management process to prevent things like that from happening (or whatever your company did). And isn't it true, that what we can do for our customers today, outweighs what we weren't able to do for them in the past?"

40. Objection: *I don't like your products/services.*

When? Early on after the prospect learns what you sell.
Probable Cause: Prospect has previous direct or indirect experience that damaged credibility.

Objective: Reestablish credibility.

Prevention Strategies:

1. In your pre-call planning phase, if you discover that a company has tried your products/services before, then discontinued, recognize that there may be some dissatisfaction you'll need to preempt.
2. Approach the prospect with new or enhanced products/services.
3. Focus on the logic presented using the FAB / TEA formula, track records and testimonials.
4. Use free trials and observation trips or video conferencing with other clients successfully using your products and services.

Preemption Strategies:

1. From your records, bring up and talk about the products they bought so you can discover how dissatisfied they are, and most important, what brought on the dissatisfaction.
2. Use the three steps to defuse negative emotions (Recognize, Apologize, and Solutionize).

Response Strategies:

1. Use Active Listening Skills to communicate your understanding of the situation that caused the customer to change suppliers. Use a transition sentence appropriate to the situation. For example, "With all that's happened, I can certainly understand why you're dissatisfied with our products." Next, problem-solve with the customer to resolve issues.

2. Orient the conversation to where you are strong, the competitor is weak, and the customer has needs with that specific product/service (Research Questions). For example, "Some really unfortunate miscommunications caused this. I want to work with you to make sure the next time you order from us, that I'm in the loop to monitor and make sure our new systems are working properly for you. When you started using our products, what attracted you to them, was it the ____ (strong USP) or the ____ (strong USP)?" Now you're in a sales conversation with them.

3. First, actively listen to make sure the prospect knows that you understand their experience. Defuse any negative emotions, and then say, "Yeah, that was an eye-opener for our company and now we've come a long way since then. Like many companies, we instituted a Total Quality Management process to prevent things like that from happening (or whatever your company did). And isn't it true that what we can do for our customers today, outweighs what we weren't able to do for them in the past?"

41a. Objection: *You don't understand our problems.* (Needs not identified)

Special note: There are three primary causes for this type of objection: 1) needs not identified, 2) not including your discovery phase in your presentation, especially with people in the room you didn't interview, and, 3) lack of understanding about their industry. Each cause will be handled separately.

> **When?** During general shotgun type presentation.
> **Probable Cause:** (41a) Insufficient diagnostic interview. Needs not identified.

Objective: Establish your credibility and right to speak. Identify needs.

Prevention Strategies:

1. Diagnose problems before you present solutions. You do this by using your USPs to guide your Research Questions and then use the FAB / TEA formula to confirm the symptoms, problems, costs, and solution specifications.
2. Make sure your solutions will fit this specific business and political environment.
3. Summarize what you learned during the Research Question phase of the process. This summary will make it clear that you truly do understand the issues.
4. As you bring up each need you've identified, use the FAB / TEA formula to present it. Use the Benefit question to establish value, trigger favorable emotions, and create attitudes.

Preemption Strategies:

1. "Before I get beyond the general introduction to our company and products, I'd like to focus on where they are normally in your specific work process." Now use your Research Questions to uncover needs.
2. "Can you give me a brief overview of how you currently ___?" Now use your USP guided Research Questions to uncover needs.
5. "Let me make sure I understand your work process in this area. As I see it . . ." Now use the FAB / TEA formula and especially the Benefit Questions to establish value, trigger favorable emotions, and create attitudes.

Response Strategies:

1. Stop presenting when you get this objection. Then, "It seems that I've missed some important concerns. Help me out. What areas do we need to focus on? What are some concerns you have in this area?"

2. "Yes, you're right. I got way ahead of myself. I'm supposed to be asking questions that would help me truly understand your unique needs. Can we roll this back and let me start over? Okay? Tell me about ___ (USP) how are you currently doing this?" Continue now with your USP guided Research Questions in the applicable areas.

3. Once you diagnose problems, determine what the problems are costing them and from what budget, then set the criteria for selecting a suitable solution that includes your Unique Selling Points using the FAB / TEA formula.

41b. Objection: *You don't understand our problems* (trust issue).

> **When?** During general shotgun type presentation.
> **Probable Cause:** (41b) Failure to present your situational analysis before the solutions phase of the presentation.
> **Objective:** Establish your right to speak (credibility).

Prevention Strategies:

1. Always make sure you use the Active Listening Skills (repeat, paraphrase, reflect, summarize, and so on) during your interactions with prospects and especially before you present.

2. Use the standard methods to establish trust and rapport and to build capability and credibility.

3. Begin any presentation with your analysis of the situation. Doing this establishes your right to speak and be heard (see "Plan of Action" close in the Step-Based Closing Strategies section).

   a. Include the symptoms and clues (missing Advantages and Benefits of your USPs) that you discovered that makes you believe this prospect has a problem you can solve.

   b. Include your quantification of what the problems are costing the prospect from their current or projected budgets.

   c. Use as many words and phrases they use themselves as is prudent. They hear them but don't recognize them as their own. To them, they seem psychologically comforting and communicate that you understand.

Preemption Strategies:

1. "Before we get deep into solutions, I'd like to review my understanding of the situation, and then we can move on to talking about the problems we identified and the costs associated with them. To begin . . ." Now discuss your situational analysis, the problems uncovered (especially those associated with your USPs), the associated costs and where that money is currently budgeted. Once this is done, you can then begin to address each problem and the solution you feel would work best for them.

2. Make a brief "credibility building" overview of your qualifications. This begins with a quick "elevator speech" in which you state what you do that is a benefit

to the listener, how you do it differently (USPs), who you do it for, and the stellar results you get.

Response Strategies:

1. Stop presenting, then, "It seems that I've missed some important concerns. Help me out please; let's narrow the areas we should focus on. Where would you like to start? What's your greatest are of concern? What gives you the headaches that take your time?

2. Once you diagnose problems, determine what the problem is costing them and from whose budget, then set the criteria for selecting a suitable solution that includes your USPs. Now you can make your presentation that should include these steps:

   a. Situational analysis: Review your understanding of their situation to provide context.

   b. Symptoms and problems uncovered: Symptoms are the missing Advantages and Benefits that point to the missing Features (problem) that provide the Advantages and Benefits. You'll always find these if you orient to and focus on your USPs.

   c. Costs associated with the missing Advantages and Benefits: This will help you substantiate the cost of the Features that provide the Advantages and Benefits.

   d. Criteria for selecting a solution and solution provider: These criteria should now include your USPs including those from the Differentiating Commodities list.

   e. Plan for Implementation: Steps that you and the customer need to do to complete the process, including getting the purchase order. Once they agree to the overall plan, you pre-closed on the sale.

41c. Objection: *You don't understand our problems* (company credibility issue).

> **When?** During general shotgun type presentation.
> **Probable Cause:** (41c) Unfamiliar with industry or company.
> **Objective:** Establish your right to speak (credibility).

Prevention Strategies:

1. During your pre-call planning, it will be clear that this is a different industry/company.
2. Call the prospect's sales department and ask them to send you information on the company and their products/services.
3. Talk with others in your company and with your networking contacts to discover if anyone has any background in this area.
4. Read industry specific magazines found in the library.
5. Attend industry specific trade and professional organizations. As an associate member, get on the membership and publications committees. Write brief articles for publication to get your name in front of your prospective customers. Use these publications as interest mailers and credibility builders.
6. Get prepared and let the prospect know the background research you have done. They will be more helpful and sympathetic with someone trying to learn.
7. Use the standard methods discussed earlier in this book on how to build capability and credibility and how to establish trust and rapport.

Preemption Strategies:

1. "Just so you know from the beginning that I'm not an industry expert, but what I do know, is how my products are applied to problems common to most industries. So as the product applications expert, let me ask a couple of critical questions to make sure, these solutions will fit for you." Now ask critical qualifying and Research Questions related to your USPs.
2. "Before I go much further, I need to spend some time learning if you need any of these 'wonderful and exciting' things we can do. Let's start with just a few quick questions so I know where to deep dive."
3. "We don't want to put a $5.00 solution on a nickel problem, so let me ask a few targeted questions so we'll know whether this is worth pursuing, make sense?"

Response Strategies:

1. If your knowledge of the company/industry is weak, then "Yes, my background (experience) is limited in your industry, however, our products/services offer some unique cost saving Advantages to our customers that I want to make sure will work for you. Could you help me, or maybe recommend someone in your company who could?"
2. "I'm the first to admit that I'm on the outside looking in. That means I may be off-target a bit so I'll need you to guide me. But it also means that I'll have some unbiased ideas, but as Thomas Edison said, 'Make it a point to keep on the lookout for novel and interesting ideas that others have used successfully. Your idea has to be original only in its adaptation to the problem you are currently working on.' So let's take a quick look at

what we're proposing so we can determine if it will achieve the results you want. Will that work for you?"

42. Objection: *Your track record isn't strong enough.*

When? Presenting your company background.
Probable Cause: Prospect does not believe you have sufficient experience to be credible.
Objective: Establish capability and credibility.

Prevention Strategies:

1. Determine the extent this prospect meets the profile of your most desirable customers in this market segment.
2. Highlight content in the information you send the prospect, the relevant experience your company has with the problems they face.
3. If no industry specific experience, then lay the foundation using the basics of related experience in similar industry.
4. Establish yourself as the product/service applications expert.
5. Emphasize that your product/service is used in so many applications across many industries.
6. Orient the topic of conversation to those workflow areas where you are strong, the competitor is weak and the customer has needs.
7. Work out a detailed plan for advancing the sale and implementing the product/service that includes beta testing, pilot projects and other critical "go/no go" milestones.
8. Use the methods to build capability and credibility and establish trust and rapport.

Preemption Strategies:

1. Wait until you've set three to five USPs as criteria for selecting a solution and solution provider and created sufficiently strong positive attitudes before going into your company's track record. "As you can tell, we are gaining experience in this area and will always be learning. What that really means is that we clearly understand the processes and have the protocols in place. We made sure to hire people with extensive experience, so even if our company is relatively new to this type project, our people definitely are not. It also means that we're flexible and can modify our approach quickly and to accurately meet your unique needs."

2. If your track record isn't strong, then you need to document every experience you do have so you can instantly discuss results. Get written testimonials. As you gain more experience, you'll want to target those testimonials to specific areas customers have had anxieties before they bought, but are now strong proponents of yours for those areas.

Response Strategies:

1. "That's a good point and I'm glad you brought it up. When we look at the implementation team, we need to be sure it has someone on it with industry experience to provide the necessary guidance. If the answers were already within the industry, you would know about them. What we're seeing is a need for innovative thinking with ideas that have worked successfully in other industries to apply to the challenges your company is facing. It's at least worth exploring the potential of this type of solution, isn't it?"

2. "While it may seem vital at the moment to find someone with the longest track record in this area, your ability to meet each phase of the project on time and within budget using a dedicated team, led by an experienced professional you know can get these results is what's going to dominate your decision, isn't it?"

43. Objection: *Had a bad experience with your company.*

> **When?** Initial contact (often not verbalized).
> **Probable Cause:** Prospect has previous direct or indirect experience that damaged credibility.
> **Objective:** Reestablish credibility.

Prevention Strategies:

1. During the pre-call planning phase, if the customer has returned product or canceled services, then be forewarned that something didn't go right. The objection will be there so you can move on to the preemption strategies.
2. For everything you do or say, be prepared to back it up with proof and action.
3. During your initial contact, discuss initiatives your company has taken to ensure customer satisfaction such as training your customer service representatives, implementing total quality management, installing new computer software contact management system, and so on.
4. Use recent testimonials about your products/services; especially ones talking about some improvement or innovation your company has made.

5. Use the FAB / TEA formula with a focus on the Benefit Questions to get the customer to make the claims rather than you.

6. Use standard methods to build capability and credibility and to establish trust and rapport.

7. Note that this is sometimes a difficult situation to detect so be prepared to respond.

Preemption Strategies:

1. If you know the customer had a bad experience, then be prepared to actively listen (acceptance responses, asking clarifying questions, repeating, paraphrasing, reflecting and summarizing) so the customer feels you really do understand.

2. The customer will be interested to hear what you've done to prevent that bad experience from happening again.

3. Be prepared to defuse negative emotions (Recognize, Apologize, and Solutionize).

Response Strategies:

1. "Tell me what happened." Most of all, the prospect wants to be heard and understood, so use your Active Listening Skills.

2. Next, use the three-step method to defuse negative emotions (Recognize, Apologize, and Solutionize).

3. Transition to the future. "We've come a long way since then." Explain what your company has done to prevent that from happening again. "While we weren't able to provide the level service you needed back then, we are now prepared to exceed those expectations, and with our partnering program, we can plan for the future

needs of our customers so we're always a step ahead. We want to earn back your business. What do you see as our next step?"

4. Propose a plan of action to earn back the business.

44. Objection: *That can't be done.*

When? After you have made unsubstantiated claims of Benefits

Probable Cause: Prospect does not believe you.

Objective: Reestablish credibility using "irrefutable logic."

Prevention Strategies:

1. Make sure your Features, Advantages, and Benefits flow is logically defined ("if this, then that"). They should make sense whether you say them backward or forward or start in the middle.

2. Emphasize the FAB logic. "If you get the Feature, then it follows that you will also get the Advantages and Benefits it provides." The container is made of plastic (F) so it won't rust (A) which means they won't need a budget (B) to replace them due to rust. Benefit Question would be, "How do you see that reducing your replacement budget?"

3. Emphasize the need to see and agree on the "logic" of the solution before looking for references or research studies.

4. Ask the prospect what Benefits they will receive from having their needs met by getting your Feature. Use the FAB / TEA formula. Tell the Feature, Explain the Advantages, and Ask the prospect about the extent they will get the Benefits. They are now making the claims,

not you. The person making the claims has the burden of proof.

5. Ask Benefit Questions. Use the "Creating Attitudes" process.

6. Use references and testimonials to support the logic. Then use Beta tests, pilot studies, free samples, and so on.

Preemption Strategies:

1. Except for your brief elevator speech, don't make claims. Allow the customer to tell you the Benefits they will get from the Feature that logically delivers them. For example, using the FAB / TEA formula, "The (**T**ell the Feature) containers are made of plastic (**E**xplain it with the Advantage) so they won't rust. (**A**sk about the Benefit) How do you see that impacting your budget for replacements due to rust?"

2. Ask a lot of Benefit Questions to establish value, trigger favorable emotions, and create attitudes.

3. Have ready references and testimonials to introduce at strategic times during your presentation in order to back up everything you say.

Response Strategies:

1. "When I first looked at this, those were my exact thoughts, and then I found out that this product/service is not quite like others on the market. It has ___, ___, and ___ (state the Features, Advantages, and Benefits of your Unique Selling Points that will if in place, provide the Benefit claim that brought on the objection)." Ask the prospect what Benefits s/he believes will happen once s/he gets your USP's Feature

and Advantage. "What Benefits do you feel you would get with these ___ (USP Feature and Advantage)?"

2. "And if I can demonstrate this using your situation, and it clearly shows the ROI will make this one of those talked about investments, can we then move on to the part where you buy it?" Use high humor. Now you've got permission to demonstrate with the FAB / TEA formula.

45. Objection: *I don't believe it.*

> **When?** After you have made a claim for Benefits the prospect will get if s/he buys.
> **Probable Cause:** Prospect does not believe you.
> **Objective:** Reestablish credibility using "irrefutable logic."

This is similar to the "It can't be done" objection number 44 above, so the prevention, preemption and response strategies will be similar.

Prevention Strategies:

1. Make sure your Features, Advantages, and Benefits are logically defined ("if this, then that"). They should make sense if you say them backward or forward or start in the middle.
2. Emphasize the FAB logic. "If you get the Feature, then it follows that you will also get the Advantages and Benefits it provides."
3. Emphasize the need to see and agree on the "logic" of the solution before looking for references or research studies.

4. Ask the prospect what Benefits they will receive from having their needs met by getting your Feature and Advantage. Use the FAB / TEA formula. Tell the Feature, Explain the Advantages, and Ask the prospect about the extent they will get the Benefits. They now are making the claims, not you. The person making the claims has the burden of proof.

5. Use references and testimonials to support the logic but only after they have been agreed to the logic.

6. Ask Benefit Questions. Use the "Creating Attitudes" procedure.

Preemption Strategies:

1. Except for your brief elevator speech, don't make claims. Allow the customer to tell you the Benefits they will get from the Feature that logically delivers them.

2. Lead with questions instead of making claims. Establish "irrefutable logic" for each USP FAB.

Response Strategies:

1. "When I first looked at this, those were my exact thoughts, and then I found out that this product/service is not quite like others on the market. It has ___, ___, and ___ " (USPs)." Ask the prospect what Benefits s/he believes will happen once s/he gets your Feature and Advantage. "What Benefits do you feel you would get with these ___ (USP Features and Advantages)?"

2. "And that's exactly why I'm here. I didn't believe it the first time either, and then my manager took me to a customer's location where it was indeed working according to plan. If you're up for a quick field trip, let me first discuss the logic of what you'll see, and then

let's go see it in action. The company I have in mind is not one of your competitors and they love showing it off. After that, let's get the other decision-makers together and take them on a field trip where you can explain it to them using your company's jargon, make sense?"

46. Objection: *I've never heard of your company.*

When? Initial Contact.
Probable Cause: Prospect has little or no information about your company's capabilities or credibility.
Objective: Build capability and credibility.

Prevention Strategies:

1. Use referrals to gain entry to a new market.
2. Join industry trade and professional groups and get on membership and publications committees. Just imagine how many people you're recruiting for membership and could get through to by saying, "Hello, I'm ____ with ____ calling on behalf of ____. Good morning." Publish a couple of paragraph length articles with most of your writing focus on your headline and byline. Members will get to know you quickly.
3. Send a corporate image brochure.
4. Identify references you can use or name drop.
5. Find symptoms of problems you can solve fast.
6. Emphasize the need to see and agree on the logic of the solution before deciding who will implement it. "If it doesn't make sense logically, it won't get the necessary internal support no matter who implements it." Once the logic is accepted, the prospect will be more open to accepting more positive feelings about your proposal.

Preemption Strategies:

1. Write an elevator speech telling who you are, what you do that is a benefit to them, who you do it for, and how you get stellar results. Then, practice, rewrite, practice, rewrite. You have ten seconds to earn two minutes.
2. "Our company doesn't spend a lot of money on brand advertising. Instead, we're building our brand on the results we help our customers get." Now quickly name a two or three clients this prospect would easily recognize as companies with high standards.
3. "We're the company in the background that ___, ___, and ___ (USPs)."
4. Run an advertisement in a periodical that your prospects read.
5. Send (or attach to an e-mail) an "Interest Mailer" to the prospects you're targeting that contains credibility building information. It should be something that by virtue of their profession or position they would be interested in seeing.

Response Strategies:

1. "I can understand your concern about doing business with a company you're not familiar with, and I believe we can quickly fix that. To start with ..." Now give your elevator speech, and then continue with your USP guided Research Questions.
2. "While it may seem vital at the moment to do business with name brand companies, in the long run, your ability to get ___, ___, and ___ (name three USP Benefits you know they want), is what's going to dominate your decision isn't it?"

3. "I know you want _____ (USP), so isn't it true that the fact that our company name isn't as easily recognized as some others, is less important to your ability to get _____ ?"

47. Objection: *You'll have to prove that to me.*

When? After you have made claims for Benefits to be received.

Probable Cause: Prospect has insufficient information or logic to draw a believable conclusion.

Objective: Establish capability to deliver and reestablish credibility.

Prevention Strategies:

1. Logic before proof.
2. Make sure your Features, Advantages, and Benefits are logically defined ("if this, then that"). It should make sense by saying them backward or forward or starting in the middle.
3. Emphasize the FAB logic. "If you get the Feature, then it follows that you will also get the Advantages and Benefits it provides."
4. Emphasize the need to see and agree on the "logic" of solution before looking for references or research studies.
5. Ask the prospect what Benefits they will receive by getting your Feature and Advantage instead of telling them. The person making the claims has the burden of proof.
6. Use the FAB / TEA formula (Tell the Feature, Explain the Advantage, and Ask about the Benefit) which gets the prospective customer to make the claims for

Benefits rather than the seller. For example, The (Tell the Feature) containers are made of plastic (Explain the Advantage) so they won't rust. (Ask about the Benefit) How do you see that impacting your budget for replacements due to rust?"

7. Use the "Creating Attitudes" process.

Preemption Strategies:

1. Use the FAB / TEA formula (explained above) to get the prospect to make the claims instead of you. The person making the claims has the burden of proof.
2. Lay out precise documentation to back any claims you might make.
3. Start with small easily provable claims and gradually move to the bigger claims. Each time, prove it before you move on. Gradually start using the Benefit Question to shift the burden of proof to them.

Response Strategies:

1. "When I first looked at this, those were my exact thoughts, and then I found out that this product/service is not quite like others on the market. It has _____, _____, and _____ (state the Features, Advantages, and Benefits of your Unique Selling Points that will if in place, provide the Benefit claim that brought on the objection)." Ask the Benefit Question. "What Benefits do you feel you would get with these _____ (USP Features and Advantages)?"
2. "It is hard to believe and if this were like the other products on the market we'd be on the same page. What's different is that . . ." Now use the FAB / TEA formula. For example, "Our product is made from

plastic so it won't rust. Now can you see why our customers don't have to worry about having a budget for replacing these due to rust?"

48. Objection: *I've never had good results with _____.*

When? After the prospect hears what you are proposing.

Probable Cause: Prospect does not believe that your products, services, and company have the capability to deliver the Benefits. Credibility is somehow tarnished. Or it could be the prospect had a bad experience with your "type" of product with a competitor's version.

Objective: Demonstrate "irrefutable logic."

Prevention Strategies:

1. If you know that the customer has been dissatisfied, perhaps by seeing a record of a returned product, then you can't prevent it from being an ever-ready objection, spoken or not. In this instance, focus on preemptions.

2. If you don't know about any previous encounter with this product, yours or the competitors, then proceed with prevention strategies as usual such as using your Research Questions and the FAB / TEA formula.

3. Assume that if this objection is a common one for you, that it might not be your product but instead your "type" of product. In that case, also become familiar with the strategies under the previously discussed Buyer Belief "Type of Solution Will Work."

4. For every claim you make, be prepared to back it up with logic, proof, and testimonials. Better to let the prospect make the claims by using the FAB / TEA Benefit Questions.

5. During your initial contact, discuss product enhancement initiatives your company has taken to ensure customer satisfaction. Focus on the weak spots or general complaints with your type of solution (yours and competitors).

6. Use testimonials about your products/services, especially recent ones, talking about some improvement or innovation your company has made.

Preemption Strategies:

1. During the pre-call planning phase, if the customer has returned product or canceled services then be advised that something didn't go right. If you can find out what went wrong before you talk to the customer, then you can lead with changes that have been made to prevent that from happening again.

2. With most products and services there are standard "wish" points such as, "I wish it would (or wouldn't) ____." Find out what they are for yours, and then lead with how your company compensates for them. For example, your company may have fixed that wish point or may have built in a "trade-off." Using a phrase of persuasion, you can structure your trade-off Benefits in an acceptable format. For example, "While none of the products in this classification offer that, what we do to compensate is to allow you to ____ (state a "big bang" Benefit). And, from what our customers say, that truly offsets not being able to ____, wouldn't you agree?"

Response Strategies:

1. Use Active Listening Skills to discover how the prospect used the product/service and the results s/he

got. Now you can diagnose the cause of the dissatisfaction and how you might be able to fix it or compensate for it.

2. Problem-solve with the customer, or if the problem is known and fixed, then discuss the fix. If the problem is not fixed but can be offset, then discuss how you compensate for it. "That's a valid objection to your application; we have several customers who have the same equipment (or process) you do, so to compensate we offer them ___ (state how you compensate)." "And while your ability to ___ is important and we can compensate to help you achieve those results, in the long run, your ability to get ___ (USP) is what will dominate your decision, isn't it?"

49. Objection: *Your _____ is not good enough.*

When? After the prospect learns what you sell.
Probable Cause: Prospect does not believe your product, service, or company has the capability to meet their needs.
Objective: Establish capability and credibility.

Prevention Strategies:

1. During the pre-call planning phase, if the customer has returned product or canceled services then be advised that something didn't go right. In this case, you're not going to prevent something because it already exists. Focus your efforts instead on preempting the objection.
2. During your initial contact, discuss product enhancement initiatives your company has taken to ensure customer satisfaction.

3. Use targeted Research Questions, and then the FAB / TEA formula to identify value, trigger favorable emotions, and create attitudes.
4. Use testimonials about your products/services, especially recent ones, talking about some improvement or innovation your company has made.
5. Note that this is sometimes a difficult situation to detect so be prepared to respond.

Preemption Strategies:

1. If you know about a preexisting problem, then lead with the fix. Most often this objection is focused on some performance issue whether its company related (deliveries, financing, lead times, customer service, and so on) or product related (speed, strength, durability, and so on).
2. For everything you do or say be prepared to back it up with logic, proof, and action. Use the FAB / TEA formula to establish standards.

Response Strategies:

1. "Several of my customers came to the same conclusion until they found out that we are providing a product/service that doesn't have all the bells and whistles found on competing products/services. We provide only what you need to reduce the potential for problems. If you need the additional capability, we supply it at that time. And, while I know you're concerned about not having all these other capabilities on standby, but wouldn't you prefer trouble free operations, over having Features that are rarely used?"

2. "Not good enough?" Allow the prospect to explain as needed, and then you'll be able to target either a direct response to provide correct information or use a phrase of persuasion to offer a trade-off.

50. Objection: *We only buy name brands.*

> **When?** After you introduce your products, services, or company.
> **Probable Cause:** Prospect does not believe that you have the same capabilities as the branded products and services.
> **Objective:** Establish capability and credibility using "irrefutable logic."

Prevention Strategies:

1. During your research, you will determine the products/services the company currently uses. Your first tip-off that "brand" may be important is by identifying a pattern. If most everything they buy is a name brand, then this objection is likely to occur, spoken or not.
2. Using the results of your Competitor Analysis, continue to orient the topic of conversation to where you are strong, the competitor is weak and the customer has needs.
3. Make sure your Features, Advantages, and Benefits are "logically" connected so it becomes a "foregone conclusion" that if the Feature is purchased the Advantages and Benefits will follow.
4. Weaken or neutralize this perceived competitor strength by pointing out early in your discussion that your

company sets a priority on investing money to ensure customer satisfaction over spending it on advertising.

Preemption Strategies:

1. Set the stage for performance and reliability. "We test each subcomponent we use. Sometimes the better product is the lesser known and sometimes we get terrible results from the better marketed product. So while we do use name brand components, we're definitely oriented toward function, performance, and durability. How do you see those qualities playing a part in your purchasing strategy?"

2. Conduct a thorough Needs Analysis and make sure your USPs become part of the specification package. Be observant to items that are not name brands. Talk about how many parts of name brand products are manufactured by obscure companies. You might use some examples of cars being assembled in different parts of the world, computers, phones and other common items being manufactured by companies no one has ever heard about. Continue with this line of thought. In the past, many name brand companies manufactured their products, but today that's rarely the case. So much of what we think is built by the name brand, isn't."

Response Strategies:

1. "Name brands do carry a lot of weight in many buying decisions because as customers we perceive that branded products have more to protect so more care is given to their production. It also means that the product/service has to have the widest appeal rather

than being narrowly focused. And that's why we're here. You have applications that are very special and in areas where we specialize. "One size fits all," in some situations just doesn't work. Some good examples in your application are ____, ____, and ____ (USPs). I know you want the right product/service for the job, so isn't it true that name of the brand is less important than getting your application right?"

3. "And we use many name brand components in building our product where they count and can demonstrate functional superiority so we've got you covered there."

4. "While using only name brand products may seem vital at the moment, your ability to ___, ___, and ___ (USPs) is what's going to dominate your decision isn't it?"

51. Objection: *You don't have what we need.*

When? After the prospect discovers what you sell by learning about certain characteristics of your product, service, or company.

Probable Cause: Prospect does not believe that your products/services have the capability to meet their needs. This is different than objection number 31, where it was a "Type of Solution" issue.

Objective: Establish capability.

Prevention Strategies:

1. Match the profile of your prospects with those of your most desirable customers.

2. During your research phase, make sure you review the prospect's workflow process to see how your products/services will work. Lay out how the current

products/services work and how you could enhance the process with your Unique Selling Points.

3. Orient the topic of conversation to where you are strong, your competitor is weak and the customer has needs.

4. Make sure the connection between your Features, Advantages, and Benefits is strong and logical.

5. Identify the problems that only you can solve with your Unique Selling Points.

6. Focus on the Advantages of your solution's Features and how they provide better Benefits (more certain, quicker, stronger, and so on).

7. Use the FAB / TEA formula to establish the solution and supplier selection criteria.

8. Use the Benefit Question to lock in the criteria and create attitudes favorable to you.

Preemption Strategies:

1. Many times, preconceived notions customers hold about your company and its products and services are inaccurate. This means that a simple elevator speech tied to their work processes will often take care of this objection.

2. Using the characteristics your customers have in common (Profile), determine the extent to which this prospect meets them (Qualify). Next, let your USPs guide your Research Questions to uncover needs you can meet better than the competition (Needs Analysis).

3. No matter what you sell, do a "needs analysis." You might find that you do indeed have what they need. And because you found Benefit deficits that only you can fill, you are positioned to meet their needs better than the competitor.

Response Strategies:

1. "I was thinking that myself, then I began to see a lot of similarities in your process and what a few of our customers use. What I suspect we might discover are the same hidden problems they had. So, if I can set aside your concern about the application issues for a few moments, let's quickly explore how you are handling ____, ____, and ____ (USPs). Which of these areas gives you the greatest concerns?"

2. Simply ask, "What do you need?" If what the customer says they want has some obvious weak spots that you can fill with your USPs, then you might say, "If you're still using those, how do you handle ___, ___, and ___ (missing USP Advantages and Benefits)? Those are constant side effects of using ___ (current method prospect is using)."

Chapter 22: Buyer Belief 8 – Best Solution

Common Objections in this Category

52. Don't see any reason to change.
53. We've got to look at a number of suppliers.
54. We've been doing business with them for years.
55. Not sure yours will work as well.
56. My brother-in-law is in the business.
57. Don't see any difference.
58. What makes you different?
59. Why should I buy from you?
60. We do it internally with our own people.
61. We want a band-aid, not a full work over.
62. It costs too much to change to your products.
63. We just like your competitor's product.

Category Overview

The prospect must believe that your solution, to the exclusion of competing solutions, will best satisfy the need.

As a general strategy for this category of objections, you would want to first neutralize the competitor's strengths to level the playing field and remove any differences between your company and your competitor's. You do this to diminish the reasons your prospect has to continue to do business with the competitor.

Next, during your Research Questions, you discovered needs the customer has and uncovered some potential holes (missing

Advantages and Benefits provided by your USPs' Features) in the current way they are trying to get the job done. You knew where to look for the holes because your Competitor Analysis identified your USPs and you used them to guide your exploration.

You then focused the prospect on these holes and using the FAB / TEA formula. You discovered that they did indeed have some unfilled needs costing them financially, subjectively, and emotionally.

Logically, if your Feature or capability is unique to your company, you know that the competitor doesn't have it. If the customer wants the Advantages and Benefits provided by your USP's Feature to fill the now identified needs, then the only way to get them is to buy your unique Feature.

The more your unique capabilities are listed by the prospect as minimum requirements, then the less likely the competitor will be able to meet those requirements. Even though the prospect may want their current supplier to remain, if they can't meet the new specifications, then they are no longer qualified. This leaves the prospect with the choice to either change the specifications or rule their current supplier out.

Unless you've got a showstopper USP, the research indicates that it usually takes three to five fully quantified USPs, providing three to five times the bottom-line difference, to be strong enough to motivate the customer to switch suppliers.

To set your unique capability's Feature as a minimum requirement, you would simply summarize the conversation with something to the effect, "So one of your requirements for a supplier would be their ability to provide you with USP FAB (state your unique selling point's Feature, explain it with the Advantage, state the Benefit in the terms the prospect used). Is that pretty much how you see it?" Or, "That makes sense, doesn't it?" End with a Rhetorical Question close such as isn't it, doesn't it, shouldn't it, and don't you agree. Using these questions will confirm agreement.

Since the FABs are structured logically, you can use any sequence that works for you. Using our plastic container example you might say, "So to get rid of the budget for replacing rusting containers and to remove the risks of transferring product, one of the minimum requirements you have for the containers you purchase is that they are made of a material that won't rust such as plastic. Is that pretty much how you see it?" Pause, then add, "And you'll also have a rust stain free warehouse for customer visits, won't you?"

The terms "specification, criteria, objective, requirement, condition, and standard" can be used interchangeably.

Prevent, Preempt, and Respond Strategies for Individual Objections

52. Objection: *Don't see any reason to change.*

> **When?** After presentation.
> **Probable Cause:** Prospect does not see your solution as sufficiently different from what they're doing now to put up with the hassle involved in changing suppliers.
> **Objective:** Help the prospect rule out your competition.

Prevention Strategies:

1. Your overall strategy is to quantifiably differentiate yourself from the competition in as many ways as possible, large and small. Start with a comprehensive Competitor Analysis so you can identify and clarify your USPs. Invest time here reviewing everything from company differences to product and service differences. Use the "Differentiating Commodities" list as a guide.

2. Convert these USPs to FABs and begin to quantify the value they have in general so you have some standards of legitimacy with which to work.

3. Align your USPs with the appropriate decision-maker role, and then conduct the FAB / TEA interview with them. This will enable you to get value quantification based on their facts and figures.

4. During your USP guided Research Questions, discover where the competitor's weaknesses are most apparent and where those weaknesses create the greatest needs for the prospect.

5. Orient the topics of conversation in areas you are strong, the competitor is weak and the customer has needs.

6. Discover problems only you can solve with your USPs and set the ability to solve the problems as criteria for selecting a product and supplier.

7. Establish the value of your USPs by asking them what it costs not to have the Features' Advantages and Benefits.

8. Set your USPs' Features as minimum specifications to select a product and a supplier.

9. Lock in these specifications by asking the prospect to tell you the Advantages and Benefits s/he and others in the organization will get.

10. Use Benefit Questions to trigger favorable emotions and create attitudes.

Preemption Strategies:

1. Usually, this objection occurs when your competitor has many of the same characteristics as your product and company. Position this as a question to the prospect, "Many of our customers look at our competing companies and don't see anything that's really different. Understandably so. The differences are not so much in our abilities to meet your central needs in this area, but rather, the major differences are in *'how'* we meet those needs. Let me explain. Here is a list of 21 ways we are quantifiably different. These differences, while seemingly small, have a very large impact on your bottom-line. Let's start at the top and work our way down the list to see how much these are costing you in your current budget."

2. Your presentation should include a situational analysis where you summarize the key findings of your needs analysis. This step establishes trust and rapport. Include the costs of the problems you found solvable with your USPs. Review each problem you solve, including those solved by the competition. Highlight those you can solve but the competitor cannot. In this step, you will show how you save or make money to offset your prices. And finally, define your plan for implementation.

Response Strategies:

1. "I can understand how you would feel that way. In fact, when I first looked at this, that's exactly what I thought,

and then I found out, that the real differences that put an undue strain the budget are directly related to the hidden collateral costs. For example, "In thinking about ___, ___ and ___ (USPs), which of these gives you the most concern?" Some common collateral costs could include such things as delivery charges, JIT inventory, locations (sometimes the delivery charges are as much as the cost of the product.). The bottom-line includes the cost to get (price of the product) plus the cost to use (efficiencies) plus any hidden costs associated with the supplier (fees, add-ons, change order fees, finance charges, and so on)."

2. "That's true, we both _____. However, there are five (number of USPs you've identified) costly differences that I think you'd like to know about that can favorably affect your current and future budgets. It's at least worth taking a few minutes to explore these differences, isn't it?"

53. Objection: *We've got to look at a number of suppliers.*

When? At the end of the presentation.
Probable Cause: Prospect wants to make sure they are getting the most input for the least output.
Objective: Help the prospect rule out your competition.

Prevention Strategies:

1. As a part of the problem-solving process, set criteria to select a product or service and a supplier that includes your Unique Selling Points (USP). Use the FAB / TEA and the Benefit Question to get the prospects to rehearse a defense the Advantages and Benefits they think they will get when their criteria are met. Create

221

positive attitudes toward your USPs. For example, using the FAB / TEA formula, "Our containers are made of plastic so they won't rust. How much savings do you see in the budget from not having to replace the containers due to rust?" Work with the prospect to quantify this amount. Then continue, "So with this much money at stake, I guess one of your criteria (specifications) to select this product, is that they're made of plastic?" With the prospect's agreement, they just ruled out competitors who don't have plastic containers.

2. At the end of each meeting, write an Action Items Plan on carbonless paper (or quickly send to them in an e-mail) with action items that both you and the prospect are to complete between meetings. This between meetings Action Items Plan is designed to block competitors and weaken the current supplier's position. See Step-Based Closing Strategies.

3. Write the criteria or specifications the prospect agreed to on carbonless paper (or send in an e-mail) so the prospect can have a copy with which to compare the competition's offerings.

4. Structure your presentation to include a situational analysis where you summarize the key findings of your needs analysis. This step establishes trust and rapport. Include the costs of the problems you found solvable with your USPs. Review the problems you solve, including those solved by the competition, but highlight those you can solve that the competitor cannot. In this step, you will show how you save or make money to offset your prices. And finally, define in standard steps your plan for implementation. This can now be used as a template with which the prospective customer can compare competitors.

Preemption Strategies:

1. Carbonless paper is a powerful tool to use when meeting with customers in person. Use it to make a list of the criteria or specifications for selecting the product, service, and supplier. Here you will be able to include your USPs as you use the FAB / TEA formula to set them as criteria. Most salespeople prefer to use a white top sheet and a yellow second sheet. They leave the yellow sheet with the prospect because it's the same color as most receipts so it won't get easily thrown away.

2. Instead of using carbonless paper, you can send the prospect the action item list in an e-mail or text message. Include the time and date for the next meeting and the list of participants. Use your e-mail program to send the meeting notice to all attendees. You can find out who the other decision-makers are when you set up the next meeting. For example, "Who else do you think should be at our next meeting?" Get the names and confirm that the prospect will check to make sure their schedules are open. Then continue with, "About how long do you think it will take to complete your list?" Then whatever they say and it's reasonable you can say, "Yes, about the same for me. So let's set our next meeting optional dates for ___, ___, or ___. And you'll check with ___ and ___ to make sure they're available for the meeting?"

Response Strategies:

1. "I can certainly appreciate that you want to make sure you are getting the best cost to value ratio. Let me make a note of the criteria you indicated were critical to

getting your needs met. That way, you can have a copy of it to compare offerings 'apples to apples.'"

2. "I'll work on these items listed on the Action Items Plan, so let's schedule our progress follow-up meeting, what date next week looks best for you?"

54. Objection: *Been doing business with them for years.*

When? Initial contact, after initial discussion and competition, is brought up.

Probable Cause: Prospect does not believe that what you have is better and/or the improvements they are aware of aren't worth the effort to change. They are comfortable with their current supplier. Note that if this comes early in the sales process, such as during the initial contact, then look to objection number two, "Already have someone" for your resolution.

Objective: Help the prospect rule out your competition.

Prevention Strategies:

1. Use the FAB / TEA formula to set your USPs FABs as specifications or criteria for selecting a product, service, and supplier.

2. Use the Benefit Question to establish value, trigger favorable emotions, and create attitudes.

3. Research indicates that it takes three to five quantified and defended USPs to get the prospect to rule out the competition.

Preemption Strategies:

1. "I know you've got another supplier that you've been doing business with for some time, and word is getting

out about several advances being made in our industry. What I'd like to do, is touch on some areas where our customers are seeing ___, ___, and ___ (USPs). If your current supplier can help you there, then great, you're good to go, but if not, then at least you'll know where you'll need to get support to benefit from these advances. Make sense?"

2. "The reason I'm calling is that I'd like to get you some written information about how we've helped our customers improve their profits by ____% with just three small changes in how they ___ (state the purpose of your product or service).

Response Strategies:

1. "That's great. How long have you been doing business with them? Did you use someone before? What made you change back then? So as I understand it, you got additional Advantages and Benefits by changing to another supplier. Things have changed so rapidly in our industry, especially in the areas of ____, ____, and ____ (USPs), that perhaps that opportunity exists again. It's at least worth taking a few minutes to explore the possibility isn't it?"

2. "They are a good company. I know them well and that's one of the reasons I'm contacting you. Our company has developed a way to reduce your operating costs in three areas using our products while increasing the level of service you get. I thought you might be interested in seeing what we've done and look at how this might impact your bottom-line. If you would like, we could set a brief meeting toward the end of next week or would the earlier part of the week be better for you?"

55. Objection: *Not sure yours will work as well.*

When? After the prospect starts to compare your product/service with a competitor.

Probable Cause: Prospect is not convinced your solution is the best solution; does not know how to compensate for your competitor's strengths.

Objective: Help the prospect see that you're as good as the competitor, and then guide the prospect to rule them out.

Prevention Strategies:

1. Use the Competitor Analysis to identify your competitor's strengths and ways to neutralize or offset (trade-offs with Unique Selling Points (USPs).
2. Use the Competitor Analysis to identify your USPs.
3. Use the FAB / TEA formula to gain acceptance for your methods for offsetting and neutralizing the competitor's strengths and for your USPs.
4. Identify problems solved by your USPs.
5. Quantify what these problems are costing.
6. Set your USPs as part of the criteria to select the product, service or supplier. Be sure to explain each point with its Advantages and Benefits.
7. Ask prospect to tell you about the Advantages and Benefits s/he (and others whose budgets this decision will impact) will get when the criteria are met. This will help lock the criteria in and make it difficult for the competitor to change it back. If there is any doubt, then use the Benefit Questions to challenge the buyers sufficiently to create attitudes favorable to you and your USP criteria.

Preemption Strategies:

1. One strategy that's been quite successful is to first gain parity with the competitor. "Yes, they do that well and have the same outcomes that we get. You made a good choice there." Next, continue building equality using your methods to neutralize the competitor's strengths. This creates the opportunity for you to use your USPs to find problems, quantify costs, and set them as criteria for selecting a solution.

2. Announce that you are both similar but with some critical differences. "We both handle that aspect of the job quite well. But, when you look at how we compare on our abilities to ____, ____, and ____ (USPs), I think you'll clearly see where we excel and provide Advantages and Benefits all for a lower impact on your bottom-line. Let's explore that further to see the extent your company will get those additional Advantages and Benefits. Sound good so far?"

Response Strategies:

1. Use your Active Listening Skills to discover the specific areas of concern, and then say, "That's true, so to compensate we ____ (state how you neutralize that strength). And, when you compare the two on ____, ____, and ____ (USPs), I think you'll agree that our ability to solve these problems more than compensates for the ____ (objection), doesn't it?"

2. "No doubt they do have a nice look, touch, and feel. And we think we do too. Now going to the next step and comparing our abilities to ___, ___, and ___ (USPs), I think you'll agree we can add so much value

that will offset the ____ they offer. It's at least taking a few minutes to explore the possibility, isn't it?"

56. Objection: *My brother-in-law is in the business.*

When? After the prospect discovers what you sell.

Probable Cause: Prospect does not believe there is sufficient difference to go through the grief of telling his brother-in-law he/she has selected another supplier.

Objective: Help the prospect rule out your competition.

Prevention Strategies:

1. Using the Competitor Analysis as your foundation, brainstorm with your colleagues, ways to neutralize the competitor's strengths and if not, how you off set them in a trade-off with your USPs. During your discussion with the prospect, point these compensating factors out using phrases of persuasion.

2. Identify problems solved by your Unique Selling Points. Here you are going to have been exceptionally attentive as to how your USPs impact the prospect's workflow processes for how they make money, reduce costs, strengthen image and lower risks (four universal business needs).

3. Use the FAB / TEA formula (Tell the Feature, Explain the Advantage and Ask about the Benefit) to engage the prospective customer.

4. Quantify what these problems are costing financially and subjectively.

5. Set your Unique Selling Points as part of the criteria to select the product, service or supplier. Explain each point with its Advantages and Benefits. For example, "So one of your requirements for these containers is

that they are made from plastic so they won't rust, and that will help reduce your replacement costs. Is that pretty much how you see it?"

6. It's also extremely important to get them to defend the Advantages and Benefits the irrefutable logic says they'll get. So ask the prospect the Benefit Questions about the Advantages and Benefits s/he (and others whose budgets this decision will affect) will get when his/her criteria are met. For example, "In addition to what we've talked about, what other Advantages and Benefits will you (or other decision-makers) get when you have this problem solved?" This will lock each of them in as minimum requirements that must be met by all suppliers.

7. Use the Benefit question to establish value, trigger favorable emotions, and create attitudes

Preemption Strategies:

1. Make multiple contacts within the company focused on the USPs you can bring to them.

2. Let your prospect know that others in your company have made contact with their counterparts and that they are in meetings reviewing some significant breakthroughs your (seller's) company has made leading to several critical competitive Advantages.

3. If it's just you, then contact the decision-maker with the relative in the business, after you've contacted other decision-makers with the USP information. Build Coaches and Sponsors.

4. Until you can provide the decision-maker whose relative is in the business enough financially impactful USPs that are set as supplier selection criteria, they will have little alternative but to stay with their relative.

Research indicates it will take three to five USPs fully quantified at three to five times the bottom-line difference for a prospect to change suppliers. With a relative in the business, you'll also need the support of other decision-makers and you may need a bigger spread at the bottom-line. And that is all very doable.

5. Let them know that you have some sample letters that others have used to gently let their current (relative) supplier know that there will be a change and the documentation for it.

Response Strategies:

1. "I can understand the potential grief that could occur if it were a personal choice. And it would make sense to meet with your current supplier to discuss how he could meet the criteria your company needs to be met to solve the problems. If they can meet the criteria, then you'll probably want to stay with them. If they can't meet the criteria, then he is saying to you that he can no longer meet your needs. That will let you off the hook while helping your company solve these problems. That makes sense doesn't it?"

2. "I certainly don't want to cause any grief in the family, but surely when you consider your company's needs and the breakthroughs that have increased your competitors ability to ___ by ___ (figure you can achieve), then it's at least worth taking a few minutes to see how this works so you're not blindsided by it, isn't it?"

57. Objection: *Don't see any difference.*

When? After your presentation.

Probable Cause: Presentation did not focus on how you will meet specific needs your competitor cannot meet.

Objective: Help the prospect rule out your competition.

Prevention Strategies:

1. Use the Competitor Analysis to identify as many differentiating factors (USPs) as you can. Most of your conversations, from your introduction to your presentation, will include these differentiating factors.
2. You'll also want to identify the ways to neutralize the competitor's strengths. If you can't make it a wash, then discuss how you can off set them in a trade-off with your USPs structured in a phrase of persuasion.
3. Identify problems solved by your Unique Selling Points.
4. Quantify what these problems are costing.
5. Use the FAB / TEA formula Benefit Questions to get the prospect to make the claims for Advantages and Benefits to be received.
6. Set your USPs as part of the criteria to select the product, service, and supplier. Be sure to explain each point with its Advantages and Benefits.
7. Ask prospect to tell you about the Advantages and Benefits they will get when their criteria are met. This will lock in your USPs as part of the criteria to select a product, service, and supplier.

Preemption Strategies:

1. One of your primary objectives in selling is to differentiate yourself from you competitor. Your Competitor Analysis is your key in doing this. So from

the moment you say, "Hello," to your presentation follow-up, you are going to be focused on your differentiating USPs.

2. Orient the customer in areas you're strong, the competitor is weak and the customer has needs (discovered during your USP guided Research Questions). By virtue of not having your USP's Advantages and Benefits, the prospect is having a problem that can be solved by buying your USP's Feature (capability). Note that they could have a way to compensate for your USP but most likely you would have discovered that during your needs analysis research (Research Questions).

Response Strategies:

1. "That's part of being "seamless" in any changeover. And when you compare the two (companies/products) on the capabilities to ____, ____, and ____, (USPs), which can be quite costly trying to deal with them in other ways, it makes sense to lower your overall bottom-line by using our product/service, doesn't it?"

2. "The reason I'm calling is that I'd like to get you some written information about how our company's new _____ is solving some costly issues related to ____, ____, and ____ (USPs). Is now a good time to quickly verify some information (brief pause), or should we set a phone appointment for later today?"

58. Objection: *What makes you different?*

When? After a generic type presentation, during an introduction at a networking event, or after you've given an elevator speech where you left out this critical element.

Probable Cause: Prospect does not see any difference or does not understand the significance of the differences.

Objective: Help the prospect recognize the differences (USPs) and the value they bring. Ultimately, you want them to use these differentiating factors as selection specifications that will in effect, rule out your competition.

Prevention Strategies:

1. After you've done a dozen or so Competitor Analyses, you'll have about a half-dozen or so strong Unique Selling Points that repeatedly show up. Use these in your opening remarks ("The reason I'm calling . . .") and to guide your Research Questions to uncover the needs for your USPs.
2. Identify problems solved by your USPs.
3. Quantify what these problems are costing using the prospect's facts and figures.
4. Set your USPs as part of the criteria to select the product, service, and supplier. Be sure to explain each point with its Advantages and Benefits.
5. Ask prospect to tell you about the Advantages and Benefits he/she (and others whose budgets this decision will impact) will get when his/her criteria are met. This will lock in your USPs as part of the criteria to select a product, service, and supplier.

Preemption Strategies:

1. Orient the topic of conversation to areas you are strong, the competitor is weak and the customer has needs.
2. Use the FAB / TEA formula to explore these areas (Tell the Feature, Explain the Advantage and Ask about the Benefit).
3. Ask quantifying questions about what it costs the prospects not to have the Advantages and Benefits of your USP's Feature.
4. On your initial contact, you could say, "The reason I'm calling is I would like to get you some written information about how our company has solved some costly issues related to ___, ___, and ____ (USPs)"

Response Strategies:

1. "On the surface, what we offer and what our competitor offers do look the same, and that's good because it makes upgrading less disruptive. Under the surface when you compare the two on their abilities to solve problems in the areas of ____, ____ and ____ (USPs), you can see a lot of differences that will help your company lower overall costs of operation, while at the same time increase productivity, and that represents a real opportunity for improvement, doesn't it?"
2. "Aside from the fact that we're able to ____, ____, and ____, not a whole lot. And that's enough to explore this further, don't you think?"
3. Use the FAB / TEA formula to quickly demonstrate your differences while at the same time engaging the prospect in defining how they will benefit from them.

59. Objection: *Why should I buy from you?*

When? After presentation.

Probable Cause: Prospect is not opposed to changing suppliers, but needs justification.

Objective: Get the prospect to recognize your differences, how those differences are important to them, and then ultimately to use those differences to get the prospect to rule out your competition.

Prevention Strategies:

1. After you've done a dozen or so Competitor Analyses, you'll note that you have around a half-dozen or so strong Unique Selling Points that repeatedly show up.
2. Identify problems solved by your USPs.
3. Quantify what these problems are costing.
4. Set your USPs as part of the criteria to select the product, service or supplier. Be sure to explain each point with its Advantages and Benefits.
5. Ask prospect to tell you about the Advantages and Benefits s/he (and others whose budgets this decision will impact) will get when his/her criteria are met. This will lock in your USPs as part of the criteria to select a product, service, and supplier.
6. Structure your presentation to include a situational analysis where you summarize the key findings of your needs analysis. This step establishes trust and rapport. Where possible, include the costs of the problems you found solvable with your USPs. Review each problem you solve, including those solved by the competition, but highlight those you can solve and the competitor cannot. In this step, you will show how you save or

make money to offset your prices. And finally, define in standard steps your plan for implementation.

Preemption Strategies:

1. "A question most people have is, 'Why should I buy from you?' And, that's a fair question. So let me answer it by telling you what I found out about your company." Start with the three highly quantifiable or emotionally laden issues you discovered with your Research Questions and the FAB / TEA formula to get the prospect to realize the Advantages and Benefits you have that your competitor doesn't.

2. "We know our customers have a choice of where they buy their _____. So let me start by saying that we're the only company who can provide ___, ___, and ___ in this area. Here's what that means to you." Now use the FAB / TEA formula to get the customer to start telling you the reasons they want to buy from you.

Response Strategies:

1. "Buying from us will provide you with the ability to solve some hidden problems related to ____, ____, and ____ (USPs) which will lower your overall costs of operation and get rid of some of those frustrations. So let's explore those frustrations and costs associated with ____ (state one USP area). Okay?"

2. "I'm so glad you asked me that question." Now use the FAB / TEA formula to get the prospect to tell you why they want to buy from you.

60. Objection: *We do it internally with our own people.*

> **When?** After the prospect discovers what you sell.
> **Probable Cause:** Prospect believes their needs are already taken care of by the internal staff.
> **Objective:** Get the prospect to rule out the competition (employees) and begin a transition to your service. Or position your service as a way to provide support to improve productivity for their internal staff.

Prevention Strategies:

1. Employees, especially those dedicated to doing what you do, are always a source of competition. However, if the staff is supposed to be doing something else and they have the responsibility to do what you do, then they can quickly become allies.
2. Target your prospecting efforts toward companies whose growth would overwhelm those doing what you do and are in need of support.
3. Instead of calling on buyers in the Purchasing Department, or even the functional area managers, you may need to be contacting decision-makers at higher levels in the organization for you to make headway where people's jobs or ways of doing business are at stake. Use prospecting contact methods such as networking (business, trade, professional, community, and charity organizations), first-class mail (logged by executive assistants), direct referrals, news releases, publishing, professional presentations, and other public-relations strategies.
4. Your Competitor Analysis will help you identify problems solved by your Unique Selling Points.

5. Align your offerings with the company's strategic initiatives.

6. Quantify what these problems are costing.

7. Set your Unique Selling Points as part of the criteria to select the product, service, or supplier. Be sure to explain each point with its Advantages and Benefits using the FAB / TEA formula.

8. Use the Benefit question to establish value, trigger favorable emotions, and create attitudes.

Preemption Strategies:

1. Once you know that your company's function is handled by internal staff, use your Competitor Analysis to identify how to position yourself.

2. Interview the customers of the internal department you're competing with to see the level of service being rendered and the challenges their customers face.

3. Target your calls to executives high enough in the organization to see the advantages of outsourcing some projects and using an external consulting firm to help the internal group stay current with changes and challenges in the industry.

4. If using employees is a common practice, then you may want to do your prospecting and positioning by networking at trade groups. This is one of the primary ways to gain access to the key people you would otherwise not be able to see without a direct referral.

5. At some point in your prospecting, you are going to need to develop internal coaches and sponsors to help you set meetings. One easy way to start to develop a coach is to simply ask, "Could you help me please?" That's hard for people to turn down. Be prepared with

the questions you need to have answered. Start with the easy ones.

Response Strategies:

1. "That's great. That will help us help you move at a more rapid pace to upgrade the systems giving you problems in the areas of ____, ____ and ____ (USPs). After you and I have explored these areas to find the facts and figures associated with how the process works, we can make a clear comparison with how, through using our products/services, you could substantially improve productivity in these areas. I would like to suggest we begin with _____ (one USP area). Or we could put a meeting together with ___ (state other people affected) to determine their priority areas. Where would you like to start?"

2. "We don't want to replace your people; we just want to provide the critical support they need where they're not expected to be equipped to handle those types of challenges and loads."

61. Objection: *We want a "band-aid" not a full work over.*

When? After you present a comprehensive program or project.

Probable Cause: Prospect does not believe your solution will best meet their current needs.

Objective: Help the prospect rule out the competition (band-aid). Or, if the band-aid is the proper solution, then become the band-aid with a plan to become the full comprehensive solution when the time is appropriate.

Prevention Strategies:

1. Brainstorm with colleagues, ways to neutralize competitor's strengths. The band-aid approach in this instance.
2. Identify your USPs relative the band-aid approach weaknesses.
3. Identify problems solved by your Unique Selling Points.
4. Quantify what these problems are costing.
5. Set your Unique Selling Points as part of the criteria to select the product, service or supplier. Be sure to explain each point with its Advantages and Benefits using the FAB / TEA formula.
6. Ask prospect to tell you about the Advantages and Benefits s/he (and others whose budgets this decision will impact) will get when the criteria are met to get the prospect to lock in the criteria.
7. Use the Benefit question to establish value, trigger favorable emotions, and create attitudes.

Preemption Strategies:

1. "At this time, we have two good options. The first is to get you up and running to meet your production objectives while exploring how to select and transition to a system that can economically meet your future needs. The key is that to save considerable money later, the solution you choose now to get things back running should be aligned with the general direction you intend to go later. Make sense to you?"
2. "What we're proposing now includes the ability to put a band-aid on the system and position you to transition to what we're proposing for the long-haul. By aligning the

systems now, you'll save significantly when you make the change. So let's start by looking at the end result and work backward to selecting the band-aid that can work to meet your needs now."

Response Strategies:

1. "That's not an uncommon reaction to our proposal. Many of our customers thought a band-aid would save money and be done in less time. And some took that path for a while before they cut their losses on the patchwork approach and decided that, while it sounded good and looked simple enough, it really wouldn't work as either a short or long-term solution. So, before a final decision is made, we should make a direct comparison with the patchwork approach and a more comprehensive approach to see which makes more sense. Let's do a quick workup of what's involved with the patchwork method and the results we can expect."

2. "I can understand that. And it may be true that a temporary fix is all you need, however, let's compare the two on ____, ____, and ____ (USPs). It may be that the temporary fix will actually take longer and cost you more and it's worth taking a few moments to explore a quick comparison of costs and results, isn't it?"

3. If the band-aid is the best approach, then, "You're absolutely right. You've got a good system and I can't see any reason to change it when all you need is a couple add-on quick fixes. We're the (not the) company to do that, and here's why." See Multi-Bid Summary Form strategy.

62. Objection: *Costs too much to change to your products.*

When? Usually, occurs after the prospect discovers the cost requirements to switch to your products.

Probable Cause: Prospect does not believe your solution is the best solution to the exclusion of competing solutions. Therefore, unlike the same objection discussed in the next category on pricing, this objection relates to the prospect not seeing any Advantages big enough to make a change. Note that the prevention, preemption and response strategies are very similar to those used for the pricing objections.

Objective: Help the prospect rule out the competition.

Prevention Strategies:

1. Use your Competitor Analysis and the Differentiating Commodities checklist to identify your top ten areas where you can be quantifiably different from your competitor. Focus on identifying subjective/emotional costs and Benefits.
2. Use this list of USPs to guide your Research Questions.
3. Use the FAB / TEA formula to quantify financial, subjective, and emotional value.
4. Use Benefit Question to establish personal value, trigger favorable emotions, and create attitudes.

Preemption Strategies:

1. "The costs associated with making any change can seem high in the short-term. But the costs of not making the change can be crippling in the long run. Let's look at these costs where they currently affect

your budgets now and where they will affect them in the future."

2. "The best time to have made this change was last year. The next-best time to make the change is now. Here's why."

Response Strategies:

1. "I will have to agree with you that on the front-end, the investment does seem a bit much and we should work with a phase-in plan. But on the downstream side, the increased productivity, operating cost savings, and improved moral will quickly offset the slightly higher up-front investment. Since we both plan to be in business this time next year, let's look at how this can be done before a final decision is made, that makes sense doesn't it?"

2. "If there were a way to roll back the clock to make this change back then, it still wouldn't help because the systems the industry had are no match for what we have today. And because change is the 'new normal,' we're recommending a modular phased in approach so should there be advancements you just can't live without, we can replace just that component of your service."

63. Objection: *We just like your competitor's product.*

When? After they've compared your product/service with your competitor's.

Probable Cause: Prospect likes certain Features your competitor's product offers. They're familiar and comfortable with it.

Objective: Help the prospect rule out the competition.

Prevention Strategies:

1. Use your Competitor Analysis information to neutralize your competitor's strengths and gain parity with the competitor. This will minimize any reasons to continue to business with them.
2. Do an extensive search for USPs using the Differentiating Commodities checklist. Here, the volume of USPs is important.
3. During your FAB / TEA interview, place emphasis on the Advantage telling how your Feature is a better way to deliver the Benefits.
4. Use Benefit question to establish value, trigger favorable emotions, and create attitudes.
5. Build a proof of concept project that rolls into a pilot that automatically beings to spread throughout the organization.

Preemption Strategies:

1. Focus on the USPs found on your Competitor Analysis and talk about them in terms that say what they avoid. What they avoid are your competitor's weaknesses. Structuring your FABs this way brings the spotlight to the competitor's weaknesses without saying bad things about them. For example, "Our containers are made of plastic (F) so they won't rust (A). How do you see rust-free containers affecting your customer's concerns about the integrity of your product (B)?"
2. Use the Change Management process and the Step-Based Closing Strategies discussed earlier in this book to incrementally move the sale forward.

Response Strategies:

1. Successful responding to this objection relies on a very honest and thorough Competitor Analysis. Brainstorming with colleagues to identify what their customers like about their products before you get hit with this objection will help you position yourself better. However, if you do get this objection at this point in the sales process, you're pretty close to losing it anyway. But do recognize that even if they do like your competitor's product better, that doesn't mean they're not going to buy from you. There might be something that would stop them from buying from your competitor such as the product is being discontinued; the company is being bought by your prospect's competitor, and so on. So if not for now, perhaps for future opportunities, you may need to ask what the prospect likes about your competitor's product. Take care not to trigger an emotional defense.

2. "Yes, they do have some nice Features, which would you say are most appealing to you?" Use Active Listening Skills to learn the Features they like, without using the challenge question, "why." "Those do make it appealing and it points out that I missed some key points in our discussion. We also offer _____ (state capability they like) but we do it a little differently. We use ___ (state your neutralizing Feature, Advantage, and Benefit)."

3. "Yes, they do have some nice Features, which would you say are most appealing to you?" Wait for prospect's response then, "Those do make it appealing, so to compensate, we _____ (state compensating factor) and when you compare the two on ___, ___, and _____ (USPs), our customers feel that the results they get from

these increased capabilities tip the scales in our favor." With this new information, could we take another look at your requirements?"

4. "Change is hard. Especially when you've done it one way for so long. We understand that. So to make sure the rollout goes well with the maximum acceptance, what we're prepared to do is . . ." See Step-Based Closing Strategies and Change Management process.

Chapter 23: Buyer Belief 9 – Return on Investment

Common Objections in this Category

64. Not in the budget.

65. Your competitor does it for less.

66. Your price is way out of line.

67. It costs too much to change to your products.

68. I can't justify spending that much money.

69. My boss will never approve it (money).

70. Your price is too high.

71. We need a better price.

72. Can't afford it.

73. You'll have to do better than that.

74. Sharpen your pencils.

Category Overview

The prospect must believe the price for the solution is less than the cost of the problem. If not, you get to hear money or value related objections such as, "Your price is too high." "We can't afford it." "I don't have the time (subjective value)."

The general strategy for this objection category is to use the prospective customer's facts and figures to determine what it is costing them financially, subjectively, and emotionally not to have the Advantages and Benefits delivered by your Unique Selling Points' Features. This is how you cost justify the price of the Feature. So buying from you will use money already budgeted, just not as much.

You will notice that many of the strategies used here were previously used in establishing other Buyer Beliefs. And by putting this Buyer Belief in place, you are, by default, establishing several other Buyer Beliefs, at least in part, including, Discomfort Felt, Need Has Priority, Type Solution Will Work, Capability and Credibility, and Best Solution. While this is true, you should be aware that the sometimes subtle differences will need to be addressed and incorporated into the strategies below to make them consistently effective for the other Buyer Beliefs you want to establish.

Prevent, Preempt, and Respond Strategies for Individual Objections

64. Objection: *Not in the budget.*

> **When?** Introducing a product/service the company has not used before.
> **Probable Cause:** Prospect does not believe there is going to be a reasonable return on investment. Prospect doesn't have this type of item in the budget.
> **Objective:** Establish value.

Prevention Strategies:

1. Use an elevator speech opening that quickly tells how you meet one or more of the four business needs by (1) solving problems with your USPs, (2) using money that's currently budgeted (just not labeled for your item), (3) pointing out that the current way is more expensive, which means you can help them reduce their current budget while getting better results.

2. "The reason I'm calling is that we just released a new ___ that is cutting our customer's budgets in this area by ___% while increasing their ___ by ___%. Could I send you the information about it or would you like to take a quick look at it online while I'm on the phone to guide you through how this is done and to answer any questions?" Ask priority Qualifying and Research Questions and move to the FAB / TEA formula.

3. Use the FAB / TEA formula to get the prospect to admit having problems solved by your Unique Selling Points. Use the model to quantify what it costs the prospect out of the current and future budgets not to have the Advantages and Benefits of your USPs. Quantify financial, subjective, and emotional costs.

4. Use the Benefit question to establish value, trigger favorable emotions, and create attitudes.

5. Ask how other decision-makers will benefit.

Preemption Strategies:

1. "The reason I'm calling is that I'd like to get you some written information about how our company has solved some costly and critical issues related to ____, ____, and ____ (USPs). The results we're getting show our clients reduced their budgets in these areas by ____%. Is now a good time to quickly verify some information (slight pause), or would you like to set a phone appointment for later today?"

2. "Most companies we do business with had the money for our products in nondescript budget categories called "cost of doing business" or "current efficiency rating," or something equally vague. So the challenge is to find the money in your current budget. The way we've done

this with our other customers is to calculate the costs associated with ___ , ___ , and ___ (USPs)."

Response Strategies:

1. "A few of my current customers came to the same conclusion until they found out that while there may not be a line item in the budget for ____ , it was definitely there but hidden in several categories in the budget called such things as ____ , ____ , and ____ (name the hidden USP cost categories). So our job is to conduct a cost-benefit analysis to determine how much it is costing you in these areas and what it will take to replace it with a lower cost solution. Make sense to you?"

2. "As a line item, it is probably not in the budget and may never be. What we don't want our product to be is a line item on the 'cost' side of the ledger. Rather we want to be viewed as a cost saver or revenue enhancer so if the inevitable cyclical cutbacks occur getting your needs met in this area is protected because we are seen as a positive impact directly to the bottom-line."

3. "True, it's not a regularly budgeted item. I'm sure buying one new tire for your car is not in your home budget, but if your current tire gets ruined, the consequences of not replacing it are just too high."

4. I understand. In fact, very few of my customers had this as a budgeted item, but that doesn't mean they weren't feeling the downside of not having it. So let's look at the budgets affected by levels of productivity, particularly in the areas of ___ , ___ , and ___ (USPs). Which of those has the greatest drain on your budget now?"

65. Objection: *Your competitor does it for less.*

> **When?** When we mention our company name (reputation precedes us) or when we state the price without first establishing bottom-line comparative data.
> **Probable Cause:** Prospect does not believe there is going to be a reasonable return on investment.
> **Objective:** Establish comparative value at the bottom-line. Change the basis of their decision from top line price to bottom-line value.

Prevention Strategies:

1. Bottom line = price to get product/service + operating costs to use + hidden costs associated with the supplier.
2. Identify problems solved by your Unique Selling Points.
3. Quantify what it costs the prospect out of the current and future budgets not to have the Advantages and Benefits of your USPs.
4. Ask the prospect what additional Benefits s/he will get with each USP to establish personal value (FAB / TEA). Extend this process to each decision-maker to establish an implied value that will benefit others.
5. Use the Balance Sheet Closing Strategy to show a side-by-side comparison of prices, use costs and hidden costs.
6. Use a Multi-Bid Summary Form in your proposal and let the prospect select the options and prices that will work best for them.

Preemption Strategies:

1. If you have a higher price to get the product or service (cost to get) than your competitor, then you know this objection will come up. You might open with, "Some people only take the top line price to get a product into account rather than the total cost of ownership. For example, some people buy cars at the lowest price point but make up for it when they realize they only get 10 miles per gallon. Paying just a little bit more would have gotten them a car that gets 30 miles per gallon so at the end of the year, with 10,000 miles driven, any guess who's paying more? That's the way it is with our products. Yes, they cost a bit more to get, but their operating costs are a fraction of what you're currently paying. Let's take a look."

2. "There's an interesting business model in which the seller literally prices their products below what it costs to make them (or buy them for resale). They do that so they can get the enormously profitable service contracts. Think about the printers you buy. They're cheap! But how much does the ink cost? And on the larger printers, you have to consider that the profit is built into the maintenance contract? We really have to look out when the price to get something is really out of proportion to what we think the value should be."

3. "Our competitor's product is a lot cheaper to get than ours, would you like to see where they're making up the difference?"

4. Use the Multi-Bid Summary Form strategy.

Response Strategies:

1. "Does it for less?" Now listen actively before adding a transition sentence and structuring your answer in your favorite phrase of persuasion.

2. "Ordinarily, when you compare just the price to get the product/service that would be my conclusion too, however, when you also look at what it costs to use it, and the hidden collateral costs associated with the company you buy from, our total bottom-line impact is much less. So what will you base your decision on, the top line price to get, or the bottom-line impact to your budget?"

3. "That's a good point I want to be sure to cover. While it seems that the top line price to get is the primary thing to consider in deciding which product to buy, that won't get you to the bottom-line unless you also add what it costs to use it. And from what we've talked about how your company operates, that's what has to dominate this type decision, isn't it?"

4. "Yeah they do it for less and this is how they do it . . ." Now explain the differences factually without negative comments or emotion. Include your USPs to further differentiate you from the competitor and to build additional bottom-line value.

5. "Oh? When all things are considered, they charge way more than most companies do. Let's take a look at what's really going on." Use the Multi-Bid Summary Form strategy to help explain.

66. Objection: *Your price is way out of line.*

> **When?** Prospect hears the price.
>
> **Probable Cause:** Prospect does not believe there is going to be a reasonable return on investment. Prospect is comparing similar products/services but is not considering the full bottom-line budget impact.
>
> **Objective:** Establish value.

Prevention Strategies:

1. Bottom line = price to get product/service + operating costs to use + hidden costs associated with the supplier.
2. Use the FAB / TEA formula to get the prospect to admit having problems solved by your Unique Selling Points. Use the formula to quantify what it costs the prospect out of the current and future budgets not to have the Advantages and Benefits of your USPs. Quantify financial, subjective, and emotional costs.
3. Use the Benefit Questions to establish value, trigger favorable emotions, and create attitudes.
4. Use the Balance Sheet Closing strategy to show a side-by-side comparison of prices, use costs, and hidden costs.
5. Use a Multi-Bid Summary Form in your proposal and let the prospect select the options and prices that will work best for them.

Preemption Strategies:

1. "When planning on making a purchase, a big question for most customers should be, 'What's included in the price?' Or maybe even more important, what's 'not' included."

2. "Let me share something interesting with you. One company charges $25 per plastic container and another company charges $10 per steel container. At the end of the year, the cheaper steel one turned out to be $10,000 more expensive than the seemingly more expensive plastic one. What are some ways this could happen?"

Response Strategies:

1. "That's just what I said when I first compared our pricing with our competitors, then I found out that the price is just the top line of the total equation. To get to the bottom-line or total cost of ownership, we also have to add what it costs to use it, and any hidden costs associated with the supplier. So let's compare bottom-lines between our products/services and your current supplier and I know you're going to be pleased." Set up the Balance Sheet Closing format. If you don't know the costs for your competitor and the prospect doesn't want to share, then just leave them blank and say, "I really don't need to know the exact numbers because from experience I know they're huge. So I'm leaving this with you to calculate your numbers so you can have a supporting document to deal with the money issues."

2. Another option is to build a sample Balance Sheet using standards of legitimacy.

3. "Out of line?" Ask the clarifying question (Active Listening Skills) and let the prospect now tell you how your pricing is out of line so you can incorporate that information into your response. When you do this you must, must, must use a transition sentence or you risk winning the argument and losing the sale because you left no options open for them to save face. Structure you answer using your favorite phrase of persuasion.

67. Objection: *Costs too much to change to your products.*

When? Prospect begins to calculate change over costs.
Probable Cause: Prospect does not believe there is going to be a reasonable return on investment.
Objective: Establish value.

Prevention Strategies:

1. Identify problems solved by your USPs.
2. Use the FAB / TEA formula to quantify what it costs the prospect out of the current and future budgets not to have the Advantages and Benefits of your USPs. Costs are subjective, emotional, and financial.
3. Pay particular attention to the bottom-line impact Bottom line = price to get product/service + operating costs to use + hidden costs associated with the supplier.
4. Ask the prospect what additional Benefits s/he will get with each USP to establish personal value (FAB / TEA). Extend this process to each decision-maker to establish an implied value that will benefit others.
5. Use one of the Step-Based Closing Strategies to define a plan that would phase in the changeover with the least disruption and lowest costs.
6. Use the Balance Sheet Closing Strategy to cast the costs into the future. Use the life of the contract or life of the product or whatever time frame and volume it takes to get the cost of changing incorporated into a lower bottom-line budget impact.

Preemption Strategies:

1. "The costs associated with making any change can seem high in the short-term. But the costs of not

making the change can be crippling in the long run. Let's look at these costs and where they currently impact your budgets and where they will impact them in the future."

2. "The best time to have made this change was last year. The next-best time to make the change is now. Here's why . . ."

3. "Before we do much more work on this, we should look at the cost-benefit analysis. We don't want to put a $5 solution to a nickel problem. So let's start by looking at _____, _____, _____, and _____ (areas that would motivate change connected to your USPs)."

Response Strategies:

1. "I will have to agree with you that on the front-end, the investment does seem high. But on the downstream side, the increased productivity, operating cost savings, and improved morale will quickly wipe out the slightly higher up-front investment. Since we both plan to be in business this time next year, let's look at how this can be done using different phase-in plans before a final decision is made, that makes sense doesn't it?"

2. "If there were a way to roll back the clock and make this change back then, it still wouldn't help because the systems the industry had are no match for what we have today. And because change is constant, we're recommending a modularized approach we can phase in to accommodate advancements you just can't live without."

3. "At first glance, that's the same conclusion I came to. Then, when I stepped back and took a bigger picture view, I found that the reduction in your cost of operation from solving some specific problems we

uncovered (USPs), would give you a payback within the year and after that, you could begin to substantially lower your budget in this area. Let's double-check my figures."

68. Objection: *I can't justify spending that much money.*

When? Prospect hears the price.

Probable Cause: Prospect does not believe there is going to be a reasonable return on investment.

Objective: Establish value.

Prevention Strategies:

1. Identify problems solved by your USPs.
2. Quantify what it costs the prospect out of the current and future budgets not to have the Advantages and Benefits of your USPs.
3. Bottom line = price to get product/service + operating costs to use + hidden costs associated with the supplier.
4. Ask the prospect what additional Benefits s/he will get with each USP to establish personal value (FAB / TEA). Extend this process to each decision-maker to establish an implied value that will benefit others.
5. Use the Balance Sheet Closing strategy to show a side-by-side comparison of prices, use costs, and hidden costs.
6. Use a Multi-Bid Summary Form in your proposal and let the prospect select the options and prices that will work best for them.

Preemption Strategies:

1. When you're meeting with a person in a buyer role such as a "Specifier" who must cost-justify their purchases, it is imperative that you conduct a cost-benefit analysis. If you don't, they face the question from their boss, "How can you justify spending that much money?"
2. Use the Balance Sheet Closing Strategy.
3. If your competitor is coming in very low, then work through the Multi-Bid Summary Form with the prospect.

Response Strategies:

1. "It does seem like a lot of money. However, when we look at the costs associated with the additional problems we've identified with your current service system (missing Advantages and Benefits of your USPs), we'll be able to find that the money is already being spent. It's just not in this budget category. Let's take a brief look at the use costs and some other hidden costs so we can identify whose budget they're coming out of."
2. "Yes, it is a lot, but it's actually less than you're spending out of your current budget and less than you'll be budgeting for next year. Let's take a few minutes so I can show you what the money is going for and you can tell me which budget area pays for it. Fair enough?"

69. Objection: *My boss will never approve it* (money).

When? Prospect hears the price.
Probable Cause: Prospect does not believe there is going to be a reasonable return on investment.

Objective: Establish value. Find the use and hidden costs in the budget.

Prevention Strategies:

1. Use an elevator speech opening that quickly tells how you meet one or more of the four business needs by solving problems with your USPs, uses money that's currently budgeted (just not labeled for your item), points out that the current way of doing what you do is more expensive, which means you can help them reduce their current budget while getting better results.

2. "The reason I'm calling is that we just released a new _____ that is cutting our customer's budgets in this area by _____% while increasing their ___ by ___%. Could I send you the information about it, or would you like to take a quick look at it online now and I'll give you a quick overview of how this works?"

3. Use the FAB / TEA formula to quantify what it costs the prospect out of the current and future budgets not to have the Advantages and Benefits of your USPs. Quantify financial, subjective, and emotional costs.

4. Use the Benefit Question to establish value, trigger favorable emotions, and create attitudes.

5. Demonstrate where they are currently spending the money.

6. Make the process as risk-free as possible.

Preemption Strategies:

1. Recognize that most purchases, unless they're routinely budgeted, don't gain easy approval in this era when companies have to show steady improvements in sales, cost controls, and profits. You'll have to quickly get the

point across that you want to propose something that will cut their current and future budget dramatically. Or something that would so overwhelmingly improve the company's image, or so dramatically reduce their risk, that they would have to consider what you're offering or risk losing their own jobs.

2. A winning strategy has consistently been to identify the money they're currently spending and the budget category in which it's located, and then compare it with what it would be if they bought your product or service. For example, suppose you're competing against a product that costs $10 and yours costs $100. But let's also suppose it takes 10 hours at $25 per hour for their contract staff to get the same results as you can get in an hour. That's $260 for the $10 solution and $125 for the $100 solution. You can now show that the labor costs are variable, current and future.

3. Bottom line = price to get product/service + operating costs to use + hidden costs associated with the supplier. Always keep this formula in mind when dealing with any objection associated with money.

Response Strategies:

1. "That is a concern that we'll want to deal with. Your boss will need to see that the money is already in the current budget, it's just not in this category. But since s/he has responsibility for the total budget, s/he will be able to see how the overall budget can be reduced by simply recategorizing the money. Let's first look at what it's currently costing you not to have ___, ___, and ___ (missing Advantages and Benefits of your USPs), to make sure our figures are accurate."

2. "Yeah, mine won't either unless I can show her how it will reduce our current spending. Is that pretty much what you're facing?" With a yes, continue to show how you can save money or increase revenues while reducing current spending. Conduct a cost-benefit analysis, and then use the Balance Sheet Closing Strategy to demonstrate where the money is really coming from.

70. Objection: *Your price is too high.*

When? Prospect hears the price.

Probable Cause: Prospect does not believe there is going to be a reasonable return on investment. Prospect is comparing similar products/services. Prospect is using an adversarial negotiating tactic.

Objective: Establish value.

Prevention Strategies:

1. Identify problems solved by your USPs.
2. Quantify what it costs the prospect out of the current and future budgets not to have the Advantages and Benefits of your USPs. Remember, bottom line = price to get product/service + operating costs to use + hidden costs associated with the supplier.
3. Ask the Benefit Question to quantify value (financial, subjective, and emotional) for each of the targeted business, human, functional needs.
4. Ask the Benefit Question to establish personal value. Extend this process to each decision-maker to establish an implied value that will benefit others.

5. Use the Balance Sheet Closing strategy to show a side-by-side comparison of prices, use costs, and hidden costs.

6. Use a Multi-Bid Summary Form in your proposal and let the prospect select the options and prices that will work best for them.

7. Negotiate standards of legitimacy that establish the numbers rather than arguing the numbers themselves. Always negotiate on principle and never give in to pressure.

Preemption Strategies:

1. The best way to preempt all the price pressure style objections is to:
   - Conduct a comprehensive Competitor Analysis.
   - Let your USPs guide your Research Questions.
   - Neutralize your competitor's strengths.
   - Conduct a cost-benefit analysis that includes your USPs.
   - Use the FAB / TEA formula to establish financial, subjective, and emotional costs for each decision-maker involved.
   - Structure the pricing part of your presentation in a Balance Sheet Closing Strategy format or in a Multi-Bid Summary format.
   - Show where the money is buried in another budget(s).

2. Unbundle your offering so you can take away what they don't want to pay for to get the price to a level in which they feel comfortable. Think about the airlines offer a basic low ticket price, and then charge extra for everything else.

Response Strategies:

1. If you've done a good job conducting a cost-benefit analysis and used the Balance Sheet Closing Strategy, then when you hear this objection you can be almost certain that it is a negotiating tactic and an adversarial one at that. The fact is that most unskilled salespeople will indeed drop their price when under pressure and often give away as much as they can the first time they're asked. Many will include the profit giveaway without even being asked. And if put under strong pressure, they will even call their sales managers and ask for more without any justification other than the customer asked. Don't do it. Take a different stance. Repeat what they said as a question, "Price is too high?" then let the customer explain so you at least have some direction to go.

2. "That's just what I said when I first compared our pricing with our competitors, then I found out that the price is just the top line of the total cost of ownership equation. We have to also add what it costs to use it and any hidden costs associated with the supplier, then we can look at the true bottom-line. So let's compare bottom-lines between our products/services and your current supplier and I know you're going to be pleased."

71. Objection: *We need a better price.*

When? Prospect hears the price.
Probable Cause: Prospect does not believe there is going to be a reasonable return on investment. Prospect is comparing similar products/services. Prospect thinks, that just because of "who they are" (name brand

company, ego), they should get preferential treatment. This is an obvious adversarial negotiating tactic.

Objective: Establish value, hold your ground to gain respect, communicate to the customer that they got the "better price," and that, without some change in the situation, there is no further discount.

Prevention Strategies:

1. A comprehensive Competitor Analysis is necessary to provide you with an understanding of what they're currently getting for what they're paying. Use standards of legitimacy if you don't know the pricing.
2. Neutralize the competitor's strengths.
3. Identify problems solved by your USPs.
4. Quantify what it costs the prospect out of the current and future budgets not to have the Advantages and Benefits of your USPs. Bottom line = price to get product/service + operating costs to use + hidden costs associated with the supplier.
5. Ask the prospect about the additional Benefits s/he will get with each USP to establish personal value (FAB / TEA). Extend this process to each decision-maker to establish an implied value that will benefit others.
6. Use the Balance Sheet Closing strategy to show a side-by-side comparison of prices, use costs, and hidden costs.
7. Use a Multi-Bid Summary Form in your proposal and let the prospect select the options and prices that will work best for them.

Preemption Strategies:

1. The prestige associated with doing business with some companies known for their high standards can help you draw highly profitable business your way. Additionally, if they can do some of the more costly services you provide, you can remove those costs and justify offering a special price. The point is that whenever you give something; always get something in return (advertising rights, reduced cost structure, referrals, testimonials, and so on). Never give in to pressure, always negotiate based on principle (high volume orders reduce your costs and you share those savings with the customer).

2. Don't keep it a secret that you want their business and what it means to you. Honesty and transparency always win when you connect your actions with your company's pricing structure. Let them know up front that you will be very price sensitive and look for ways to save costs at every turn. Don't give anything away without getting something of perceived equal value in return or you risk losing their respect and you risk setting up even harder negotiations the next time around. No one wants to leave money on the table. Once they know your walk away point, and you stand firm, then they feel they've gotten the best price they're going to get, and will move on to the purchase and implementation.

Response Strategies:

1. "I can understand you wanting to lower the top line of the overall cost equation and I think by using our products/services at this level, you will significantly

lower your bottom-line. Let's take the operating costs over 12 months, and then add the price to see how much we can lower your bottom-line compared with your current methods." Structure in a Balance Sheet Closing Strategy format.

2. "Since we do business with your competitors as well, we are not allowed to give one customer a competitive advantage over another. But what I can do, with greater access into your organization, is to find areas we could help you gain greater efficiencies." When you say, "no," you are creating a loss situation for the prospective customer and part of the loss (grieving) process is anger. So whenever you have to say "no" you will upset the customer especially if they're vested in getting some concession. Anytime you tell someone "can't" always follow it up immediately in the same or next sentence with what you "can do" and there is always something you can do.

72. Objection: *Can't afford it.*

When? Prospect hears the price.
Probable Cause: Prospect does not believe there is going to be a reasonable return on investment. Prospect is comparing similar products/services. Prospect does not have enough money to allocate to this purchase.
Objective: Establish value.

Prevention Strategies:

1. Use the FAB / TEA formula to get the prospect to admit having problems solved by your Unique Selling Points. Use the model to quantify what it costs the prospect out of the current and future budgets not to

have the Advantages and Benefits of your USPs.
Quantify financial, subjective, and emotional costs.

2. Use the Benefit Question to establish value, trigger favorable emotions, and create attitudes.

3. Show a side-by-side comparison of the costs associated with both products in a Balance Sheet Closing Strategy format. You can also cast these figures into the future. For example, suppose you have a three-year service agreement. If so, run the numbers out three years to show an even greater spread of costs.

4. Understand the prospect's financial condition. It may actually be that they may want it but truly can't afford it. For example, they may want a luxury car or a mega-yacht, but they just don't have that in the budget. Accept it and move on. Take a look at your customer profile qualifying questions to see if there is something you missed or could be adjusted to catch these prospects early in the process.

Preemption Strategies:

1. Some companies truly can't afford to pay for what you sell but the loss without your product could be catastrophic. Look at insurance as an example. A wealthy company could afford some relative size loss and while inconvenient, it would not be a disaster. Whereas, any loss of almost any size could wipe out a struggling company. It's a balancing act and this needs to be a part of the discussion. Perhaps the goal could become to use available resources to mitigate part of the risk so that a loss could be survived.

2. Provide financial investment options if they cannot pay cash for the purchase. This should be part of the discussions and phrased to make it the standard action

so they are not embarrassed. Any time you're dealing with this type of situation, you must help them save face or they won't be able to do business with you even if they wanted to.

Response Strategies:

1. "Initially, it appears that would be the case, however, from what I can tell at this point, it seems that you're spending more than this now. You may have more than enough money budgeted; it's just not in this category. Let's check to see what it's costing you out of your current budget not to have ____ (Advantages and Benefits of USPs)."

2. "I can certainly understand how you feel. In fact, some of my other customers in similar financial condition felt that way too until they found out that for companies with more money available, having something go wrong would be a big inconvenience but not sink them. But for companies in your financial condition, a loss could be catastrophic. Let's take another look at the consequences of not taking some sort of action and see if we can't get to a decent counterbalance that would reduce as much of the risk as possible without breaking the bank, make sense?"

73. Objection: *You'll have to do better than that.*

When? Prospect hears or sees the price.
Probable Cause: Prospect does not believe there is going to be a reasonable return on investment. Prospect is comparing similar products/services. It could also be someone using the legendary negotiating tactic of Henry Kissinger, "Is this the best you can do?" Note

that this specific objection is often an adversarial negotiation ploy. If the prospect says these exact words, "you'll have to do better than this," or they ask, "Is this the best that you can do?" then they have been through an adversarial negotiating course. This is the tactic Henry Kissinger used to get the best level of work Ambassador Winston Lord could provide. Don't fall for it. Follow the standard price objection prevention strategy and stand your ground. Do not give in to pressure or you'll pay dearly every time you try to sell to them.

Objective: Establish value.

Prevention Strategies:

1. Use the FAB / TEA formula to get the prospect to admit having problems solved by your Unique Selling Points. Use the model to quantify what it costs the prospect out of the current and future budgets not to have the Advantages and Benefits of your USPs. Quantify financial, subjective, and emotional costs.
2. Use the Benefit Question to establish value, trigger favorable emotions, and create attitudes.
3. Use the Balance Sheet Closing strategy to show a side-by-side comparison of prices, use costs, and hidden costs.
4. Use a Multi-Bid Summary Form in your proposal and let the prospect select the options and prices that will work best for them.

Preemption Strategies:

1. Use the standard prevention strategies as the foundation with any of the price pressure objections.

2. Include statements such as, "If there's a way for us to save costs for you, we'll definitely do it and pass it on." Or "We're constantly looking for ways to save our customers money. Doing that is just a part of the way we do business." Or "I know you're doing what you can to try to get the price down, but we're already at that point. Our focus is always trying to get the best price and value for our customers from the moment we engage with them."

Response Strategies:

1. Use Active Listening Skills such as repeating, asking clarifying questions, paraphrasing, and so on, to find out which area needs improvement. It may not be the price, but, if it is, then respond with, "I know you've got to ask, and I guess we could have added 'negotiating money' to the pricing but we would rather focus our efforts on getting the best results for the dollar. Cutting any further will mean we will have to cut something out. If you're now fine with what we're proposing, then let's move forward, if not, and you want to get the price down further, let's go through the proposal item by item to see which areas you would like to see cut."

2. "Do better than that?" If it is price then, "It certainly would be nice if we could, but as you can tell by the cost breakdowns, we went into this looking for ways to provide you with the best effort we can make. There may be some items that could be removed or perhaps some that you could assign staff to do internally that might result in a lower overall price, but I've got to say, there's not much left to take out. Have you found any

areas that you think might not be necessary as a part of this project?"

74. Objection: *Sharpen your pencils.*

When? Prospect hears the price.

Probable Cause: Prospect does not believe there is going to be a reasonable return on investment. Prospect is comparing similar products/services. This is also another standard adversarial negotiating tactic taught in some courses.

Objective: Establish value using the standard methods to prevent price pressure.

Prevention Strategies:

1. Use the FAB / TEA formula to get the prospect to admit having problems solved by your Unique Selling Points. Use the model to quantify what it costs the prospect out of the current and future budgets not to have the Advantages and Benefits of your USPs. Quantify financial, subjective, and emotional costs.

2. Use the Benefit Question to establish value, trigger favorable emotions, and create attitudes.

3. Use the Balance Sheet Closing strategy to show a side-by-side comparison of prices, use costs, and hidden costs.

4. Use a Multi-Bid Summary Form in your proposal and let the prospect select the options and prices that will work best for them.

5. Note that this specific objection is often an adversarial negotiation's ploy. If the prospect says these exact words, then they have been through an adversarial negotiating course. Follow the standard price objection

prevention strategy and stand firm to pressure tactics such as these. If there is a principle involved such as increased volume, longer lead times, and so on, you can use that principle to negotiate the reduced costs to you and share those with the buyer. Use the strategy of negotiating the standards by which value is determined rather than arguing about the end result.

Preemption Strategies:

1. First order of business is to make sure you've worked the numbers in the appropriate manner and didn't pad them so you can drop your price when the buyer puts on the pressure. If you have a reputation for dropping your price, then each consecutive time you go in to negotiate an order, your buyer must continue to exert price pressure. It's what you've trained them to do. They've always gotten concessions from you in the past using pressure. If this is the case, you'll need to retrain your buyers.

2. Let the buyer know that you really put the time in to make sure you got them the best pricing you could.

6. Use the Balance Sheet Closing Strategy to show a side-by-side comparison of prices, use costs and hidden costs.

7. Use a Multi-Bid Summary Form in your proposal and let the prospect select the options and prices that will work best for them.

Response Strategies:

1. "We really value your business, so from the start, we used the sharpest pencils we've got to make sure we give you the best bottom-line result. This means we

took the price on the top line and added the cost reduction components to produce the big dollar savings on the bottom-line. I guess we could have added 'negotiating money' to the pricing structure but we would rather just focus our efforts on getting the best results for the dollar. Cutting any further will mean we will have to cut something out. What areas would you like to see cut?"

2. "I know getting the lowest price seems paramount at the moment, but isn't getting ___, ___, and ___, that lower your related expenses, going to dominate your decision?

Chapter 24: Buyer Belief 10 – Plan Will Succeed

Common Objections in this Category

75. No one will use it.
76. Can't see how we could implement it.
77. Too much risk.
78. Change is tough to do around here.
79. Too much trouble.
80. They will never buy in to it.
81. I'm not comfortable with this idea yet.
82. This is a lot to think about.
83. They will resist doing it.
84. We need time to adjust to this.
85. Don't know how to tell my supplier "no."

Category Overview

The prospect must believe your plan to meet their needs will be successful. If not, you will hear objections such as "I don't think this will work for me" or "It's too much trouble to change."

Having an experience (direct or indirect) with a bad implementation evokes an abundance of caution. Many of these are not inexpensive failures. You'll need to make sure you've built strong corporate capability and credibility, along with strong personal trust and rapport.

Review the "Step-Based Closing Strategies" and the "Change Management" process. Build into your sales model the components from these processes you need to prevent this category of objections. Remember, the greater the anxiety and/or the higher the risk, then use smaller steps and include more feedback steps.

Prevent, Preempt, and Respond Strategies for Individual Objections

75. Objection: *No one will use it.*

> **When?** After the presentation or demonstration.
> **Probable Cause:** Prospect does not believe the plan will succeed.
> **Objective:** Provide a detailed plan for implementation.

Prevention Strategies:

1. Use a detailed, comprehensive checklist of action items that must be done in order to implement your solution. Include contingencies on your list to lower the prospect's anxiety.
2. Write on carbonless paper, or in a follow-up e-mail, the action items that must be completed by both you and the prospect between calls to continue to advance the sale.
3. Use a detailed plan of action at the end of the presentation. Be sure to include points to provide feedback to the customer.
4. Develop a standardized plan for implementation with emphasis on critical steps that prospects have raised concerns. Be prepared to tell brief stories about specific customers who had concerns in the same areas as your prospect and the stellar results they got.

5. See Step-Based Closing Strategies.

Preemption Strategies:

1. "The research indicates that ____% of these types of implementations don't achieve the sought after and promised Benefits. In fact, ____% fail. Now let me review why this happens and what we're helping our customers do, to counter these factors. With this information and our proprietary guide for implementation as a foundation, we'll create a custom plan that will meet precisely with your needs and we'll provide a list of signs and solutions to monitor during the four critical stages. Given the return on investment assigned to this project, it is well worth this extra effort to ensure success."

2. "There's a lot involved in making this implementation work smoothly. Fortunately, we have experience making sure that will happen for you. Once we get most of the big items identified and out of the way, we can then start on the 'make or break' details using our proprietary list of action items as a guide."

Response Strategies:

1. "Under normal circumstances, that would be my concern too. However, your requirements are not being met and that's costing you dearly every month it doesn't get fixed. That's why I believe it is well worth the time and effort it will take for us to customize our standard plan in a way that will give this project the highest probability for success. Let's begin by identifying all the reasons you think might be thrown

our way so we can develop ways to prevent, preempt, and respond to them."

2. "That is a good point and a critical one too. We need to plan carefully to ensure that we get buy-in from the formal and informal leadership. That means we will want to get them involved pretty early in the process. Let's make a list of people who will need to support this project to make sure it works, and then let's determine when and where in the overall plan they should be brought in. Without their participation, I certainly agree this could be stopped no matter how beneficial the project is. So, let's start with our list of key influences, what their concerns might be when to involve them, and how we might do that."

76. Objection: *Can't see how we could implement it.*

When? After the presentation or demonstration.

Probable Cause: Prospect does not believe the plan will succeed. Prospect doesn't believe the necessary resources (time, personnel, expertise, equipment, and so on) are available to be successful.

Objective: Develop a detailed plan for implementation with the prospect's input. Include the necessary resources.

Prevention Strategies:

1. Use a detailed, comprehensive checklist of action items that must be done to implement your solution. Include contingencies on your list to lower the prospect's anxiety.

2. Write the action items that must be completed by you and the prospect between calls on carbonless paper or send it in a follow-up e-mail.

3. Use a detailed plan of action at the end of the presentation. Be sure to include points to provide feedback to the customer.

4. Identify the usual resource deficiencies found in other implementations and include them in the plan.

5. Structure the plan such that one step triggers the next step which then triggers the next step with feedback and backup plans included as needed.

6. Hold a brainstorming session with the prospective customer's team and your project managers to identify the steps and backup plans.

Preemption Strategies:

1. Use words that paint a picture to help the prospect see getting and using what you sell. For example, suppose you're selling a piece of equipment you might ask, "Well you've seen the pictures and know the dimensions, but from what I can see standing here in your office, I'm not sure where you'd put it?" When they respond, "Oh, we'll move that cabinet into the copy room and put a table in the corner to hold it." You know at that time, they've mentally taken ownership.

2. "One of the key questions our customers have is about how they would implement this, especially since you are short staffed. Here's how we propose to handle that . . ." Now explain your plan.

3. Steps in the prevention strategies also apply here.

Response Strategies:

1. "The plan on how to implement it is a little fuzzy. However, given the amount of money that it is costing you each month your requirements are not being met, I believe it is worth the time and effort for us to create a detailed a plan of action that will assure success."

2. "Yes, that's where we are now in the process. Our next step is to detail the plan for implementation. What I would propose is that we start with our standard plan that we've used successfully in many other companies similar to yours, and go over each step to decide which ones will need to be done and which ones we can scratch off the list. As we're doing this, we can insert any additional steps you feel necessary, so let's begin with the major strategy steps."

3. "The project is too important to be left to chance, so let's put together a team of people from your company and mine to brainstorm all the issues and steps that need to be considered and resolved. That way we'll all be on the same page when it's time to implement. From our company, I would include our project manager and the product manager. Who should be a part of this initial team from your company?"

77. Objection: *Too much risk.*

> **When?** After the presentation or demonstration.
> **Probable Cause:** Prospect does not believe the plan will succeed.
> **Objective:** Create a detailed plan of action with the prospect's input.

Prevention Strategies:

1. Use a detailed, comprehensive checklist of action items that must be done to implement your solution. Include contingencies on your list to lower the prospect's risk and subsequent anxiety.
2. Write the action items that must be completed by you and the prospect between calls on carbonless paper or send it in a follow-up e-mail.
3. Use a detailed plan of action at the end of the presentation. Be sure to include points to provide feedback.
4. During your review of the plan, ask questions about how the prospect will implement each step. This will help you identify where the prospect is uncertain that could lead to this objection. Focus your support in these areas.

Preemption Strategies:

1. "Before we go much further, can we talk about the implementation steps that could be troublesome? I want to make absolutely certain that when you decide to move forward, this will work according to plan. Make sense?"
2. "There are three (or whatever number) steps critical to getting the highest level results possible, these are ____, ____, and ____. Let's talk about how to get these done within your organization." Now you can talk without the emotional charge of an objection clouding your ability to develop a plan that will work for this prospect.

Response Strategies:

1. "Given where we are now in the process, it does seem there are a lot of risks to consider. Any venture undertaken without a well thought out and repeatedly tested plan is high risk. Our next step would be to review our standard plan of action to make sure every step is doable in your operation. Then we can evaluate the risk-reward formula with a high degree of confidence."

2. "Just like taking a trip to someplace you've never been, downloading the detailed directions seems to increase comfort levels. And that's what we've done with our customers who find themselves concerned about how to implement this project. We've got the detailed directions to get it right. We start with a review of the steps on our standard plan to make sure they are solid and will work in your operation. Then, and only then, can a straightforward evaluation of the actual risks be made. And I have to tell you, if the uncertainty is still there, then we don't want to move forward because our reputation for delivering great results is on the line."

78. Objection: *Change is tough to do around here.*

When? After the presentation or demonstration.

Probable Cause: Prospect does not believe the plan will succeed.

Objective: Develop a detailed plan of action with the prospect's input that includes the basic and advanced change management steps and a basic understanding of how and why those steps work.

Prevention Strategies:

1. Use a detailed, comprehensive checklist of action items that must be done to implement your solution. Include contingencies on your list to lower the prospect's anxiety.
2. Write the action items that must be completed by you and the prospect between calls on carbonless paper or send it in a follow-up e-mail.
3. Talk about "change management" processes.
4. Use a detailed plan of action at the end of the presentation. Be sure to include steps to provide feedback and steps that can move forward without the prospect's input.
5. Put together a team of people from your company and the prospect's company to brainstorm the steps needed. Provide a master list of steps as a guide.
6. See Step-Based Closing Strategies.
7. See Change Management Process.

Preemption Strategies:

1. Change can be difficult anywhere, even when it's desirable for those who need to make the change. If what you sell requires a significant change, then build change management processes into your discussion. For further clarification on how this is done, see the discussion about the Change Management Process provided earlier in this book.
2. After several sales attempts and implementations (successful or not), you will know where the pitfalls are located and even some signs that tell you that you're about to encounter one. Spend time with your peers and management discussing ways to mitigate these issues.

There has to be a way to do this or no one would buy what you sell. Find the ways. Maybe it's in the profile of the prospect, or the sequence of whom to see first, or in the marketing materials that help them see themselves as change agents for the better. Whatever it is, it's there.

Response Strategies:

1. "Yes, you do have some challenges in this area. Change management procedures tell us that we have six interrelated things to do. The change management process suggests that we:
   - Show them that the current way is not the best choice to meet the company's objectives and initiate discussions of a different way currently under consideration that would get better results. Create the gap (need).
   - Ask those involved in the change, what they find good about the new way's benefits. Help them see themselves already having and enjoying this new product/service.
   - Talk about what will change and what won't change. Challenge them to find the benefits in the change, especially how change solves specific problems and removes ill-effects of not changing (Support, Challenge, and Support).
   - Discuss support, training, supervision and other resources available.
   - Engage them in developing ways on how they will implement each change.
   - Develop and agree on a clear path and plan to get the changes they now want.

The sequence can change as needed. If that makes sense to you, let's put the change management steps in the overall plan. The bonus is that you can use these principles and steps for other changes you're making in your business."

2. "That's a good point. Change can be difficult. But this isn't the first time we've done this. With your help, we can develop a custom plan that covers the steps and contingencies you'll need to influence the mental and behavioral change necessary to get the level of Benefits that make this well worth the effort."

79. Objection: *Too much trouble.*

When? After the presentation or demonstration.
Probable Cause: Prospect does not believe the plan will succeed. Could also be "too much hassle" if there is not enough discomfort felt, see objection number 19.
Objective: Develop a detailed plan of action with the prospect's input that makes it as simple and easy as possible and still get the targeted results.

Prevention Strategies:

1. Use a detailed, comprehensive checklist of action items that must be done to implement your solution. Include contingencies on your list to help lower the prospect's anxiety.
2. Categorize the steps by milestones so they recognize that the implementation will be successful but not as troublesome as they might think.
3. Write the action items that must be completed by you and the prospect between calls on carbonless paper or send it in a follow-up e-mail.

4. Discuss your detailed plan of action at the end of the presentation by categories or milestones. This way they see that you have the details, but that they will be able to manage the process at the milestone level. Be sure to include steps to provide feedback.

Preemption Strategies:

1. Simplify, simplify, simplify! Managing almost any change can get as complicated as you let it. Use terminology that your prospect understands rather than industry jargon. Explain terms not commonly used. Use logically sound and easy to understand examples.
2. Talk results and outcomes rather than the intricately detailed steps required to get them. Group the detailed steps into higher-level categories, stages or phases. Use flow diagrams. Easy to read checklists. Follow "slide show" presentation guides of no more than eight words per line and no more than eight lines per slide. Use graphs and graphics.
3. Use visual words and descriptions to help the prospect see themselves carrying out the higher-level steps.
4. Let them know that they will have constant support.
5. Let them know you have the detailed plans and expertise to do the "heavy lifting" during the implementation process.
6. "This seems to be a good time for me to point out, that while this may look like a lot of trouble, the amount of money this problem is costing you each month your requirements are not being met, is far more than the effort it's going to take to fix it. Let's start with our standard plan where we've already identified the key steps, and then custom fit it to your application."

Response Strategies:

1. "It does seem like a lot of trouble. However, given the amount of money it's costing you each month your requirements are not being met, I believe it is worth the time and effort for us to detail out a plan of action that will ensure success. Let's start with our standard plan where we've already identified the key steps, and then custom fit it to your application."

2. "Yes, it does take some effort, but I've done this many times. It's a lot less daunting than it looks."

3. "It can seem that way for sure. But in reality, it's much easier to do than it is to talk about it. For example, look at this group of steps. What that really does is . . . (summarize)."

4. "Yes, at this level of detail, we're down in the weeds where everything looks like a lot of trouble. So let's take it to the next higher-level view looking at the steps without the substeps. At this level, we can understand what's required but can move along at a more comfortable pace. If there are questions, we can drop back down to get the clarifying information." Note that if you're at the executive level, they are most interested in what's called the "30,000-foot view." So move up to the milestones, stages or phases level of the project. Provide the backup detailed steps in the handout package so they can see that you do have the details and depth necessary.

80. Objection: *They will never buy in to it.*

When? After the presentation or demonstration.
Probable Cause: Prospect does not believe the plan will succeed.

Objective: Emphasize the steps in your detailed plan of action how you get the buy-in from staff.

Prevention Strategies:

1. If getting buy-in from others is a critical part of getting the results the prospect is looking for, then it would make sense for you to develop a plan for making that happen. Include alternative plans as well that will get the same or similar results.
2. Write the action items that must be completed by you and the prospect between calls on carbonless paper or send it in a follow-up e-mail.
3. Use a detailed plan of action at the end of the presentation. For most steps, you can talk at the milestone level. Where you know buy-in will be an issue, then talk about the ways to engage staff to get the degree of buy-in necessary to get the results you and the prospect want to achieve. Be sure to include steps to provide feedback on the progress being made so midcourse corrections can be made.
4. Use the change management process to prevent fear-based objections and lack of engagement based resistance.

Preemption Strategies:

1. "Next, we need to discuss standard ways we use to get buy-in. While we're doing that, we can make any modifications to ensure it will work with your team."
2. Ask the team members questions to determine how hard it will be to get buy-in from their teams. For example, "Tell me about your team and how well they accept change. What do you think might be a good way to get

them to buy into this?" Offer up some ideas that you've used successfully in the past with other companies. Develop your plan from there.

Response Strategies:

1. "Who else needs to buy in?" Or "Who might hold back?" Now that you've got the right people identified, you can get into discussions about what might prevent them from buying in. Once you know that, you can move to identifying ways to get them to become supportive.
2. "That's not an uncommon challenge with this type of proposal. The alternative is to let things continue to run their course until you reach a crisis. However, having faced this challenge many times before, we do have a standard detailed, comprehensive plan of action to help smooth the way and get buy-in. Let's review the steps to see how this will work with your staff."

81. Objection: *I'm not comfortable with this idea yet.*

When? After the presentation or demonstration.
Probable Cause: This objection refers to the plan to implement rather than the product/service itself. Prospect does not believe the plan will succeed.
Objective: Develop a detailed plan of action with the prospect's input.

Prevention Strategies:

1. Use a detailed, comprehensive checklist of action items that must be done to implement your solution. Review this plan with the prospect and get their input. Go see

the people involved in the process, to ensure you have their input and buy-in. Include contingencies on your list to lower the prospect's anxiety.

2. Use Step-Based Closing Strategies such as the Master Plan for Implementation, Agenda, Action Items Plan, Plan of Action, Triggering Events, and the Operating Plan.

3. Use a detailed plan of action at the end of the presentation. Be sure to include points to provide feedback. Make comments along the way about the people you talked with that provided information on what needs to be done to make the plan successful.

4. Use the Change Management Process to prevent fear-based objections and lack of engagement-based resistance.

Preemption Strategies:

1. If the steps you take seem too big or rushed, then the cautious person will want to slow to a more comfortable pace and begin to find the areas that are causing the prospect's anxieties. Once the areas of discomfort are discovered, understood and accepted, then they will usually move forward. Take your time with these prospects. It will be obvious if they seem suspicious, skeptical, reserved, or uncertain in their mannerisms. They will not be rushed into a decision unless there is an incredible urgency and they have a lot of trust in you. Make sure you know which trust and rapport techniques you're using and how to read the results you're getting from these.

2. Take a look at your sales process to make certain that you have the necessary feedback steps along the way. These steps are often identified as "go, no-go" steps

somewhere toward the end of a stage of phase. If you move from one phase to another without getting the positive "go ahead" from the prospect, then you will most likely elicit this objection.

Response Strategies:

1. "This is a departure from your normal routine and so it does take some time to get used to it. To help in the process, we've developed a comprehensive plan of implementation that includes some contingencies at the critical milestones. Let's review the plan so you can get a broader perspective on how this plays out. This will go a long way to increasing comfort levels for all concerned."

2. "I can certainly understand how you feel. You've picked up on something I might have missed or that we didn't get to discuss as thoroughly as we should, so let's step back for a moment and review each component. Let's start with what we discovered during our needs analysis."

82. Objection: *This is a lot to think about.*

When? After the presentation or demonstration.
Probable Cause: This objection relates to the plan itself rather than the product/service. Often, this is related to the number of people who have to be involved and the various uncertainties this usually produces. At this point, the prospect does not believe the plan will succeed. There are too many unknown or fuzzy variables, way too detailed, not detailed enough, unduly complex, or involves many moving parts that need to be thought through.

Objective: Develop a detailed plan of action with the prospect's input so they understand each step.

Prevention Strategies:

1. Use Step-Based Closing Strategies such as the Master Plan for Implementation, Agenda, Action Items Plan, Plan of Action, Triggering Events, and the Operating Plan.
2. While you may talk at the milestone level of generality, be sure to make available a detailed plan of action at the end of the presentation that you and the prospect have reviewed.
3. Use the Change Management Process to prevent fear-based objections and lack of engagement-based resistance.

Preemption Strategies:

1. Start with your list of key or critical points that the prospect must understand and accept, to fully benefit from your product or service. Ask questions about their understanding of each of these points along the way. Try to limit these areas to five, plus or minus two, chunks with no more than five plus or minus two data points in each chunk. The research suggests that's as much as most people can comfortably process. Once you exceed this, you'll most likely elicit this objection.
2. "We're now at a point where it can be easy to get overwhelmed, so let's step back and review each segment that we've discussed to make sure we haven't missed something that could trip us up later. Let me very systematically touch on each critical point to make

sure we're both seeing it the same way. So let's start with . . ."

Response Strategies:

1. "The size and significance of the project deserve a lot of thought. And to make sure we don't miss anything in this process, we've developed a standard plan for implementation that details the steps involved. This plan will help clarify our thinking and make sure everyone concerned feels comfortable. There's simply too much at stake not to. So let's start with . . ."

2. "It is a lot to think about. So as long as I'm still here and can provide you with the answers to the questions you might have, let's review the steps and stop where clarification is needed." Now start with each major segment or cluster of steps, do a quick summarization, and then ask the prospect what needs to be added to that area. Make sure there is a "go, no-go" and a "feedback step" in each cluster.

83. Objection: *They will resist doing it.*

When? After the presentation or demonstration.

Probable Cause: Prospect does not believe the plan will succeed. This might also be related to the missing Buyer Belief, Discomfort Felt and the objection "We won't use it."

Objective: Develop a detailed plan of action with the prospect's input with a focus on the Change Management Process for the implementers and for engaging those affected by the change.

Prevention Strategies:

1. Use a detailed, comprehensive checklist of action items that must be done to implement your solution. Include contingencies on your list to lower the prospect's anxiety. Emphasize the "buy-in" steps that include in the presentation to those who are to be involved and affected what's in it for them.
2. Emphasize how you engage those involved in the change.
3. Incorporate the Change Management Process to prevent fear-based objections and lack of engagement-based resistance.
4. Use a detailed plan of action at the end of the presentation. Be sure to include points to provide feedback and "go, no-go" steps.
5. As appropriate, use other Step-Based Closing Strategies such as the Master Plan for Implementation, Agenda, Action Items Plan, Plan of Action, Triggering Events, and the Operating Plan.

Preemption Strategies:

1. When you're asking for change, especially when you're not offering anything significant in return, you can expect this objection to be lurking below the surface. Your best chance for preempting it is to focus on the outcomes the implementers or those affected by the implementation, will get regardless of how small or insignificant. Emphasis should be on how it will help their internal or external customers get their needs met, and how it will help them do their jobs better, quicker, and easier.

2. Include those affected in the process from as close to the beginning as possible. The more they are involved, the less they will resist. They may not have control over the outcomes, but they may have control about how those outcomes are reached (or vice versa). Each person needs to:
   - feel some control over what's happening
   - know that what they say matters
   - feel appreciated for the contributions they are making
   - feel they have the opportunity for input
   - understand that not everybody's recommendations can be implemented

3. "Resistance is a natural human reaction to change. We all experience it. It provides a feeling of protection until we understand the 'what, why, and how' for the change. That's why we incorporate the change management process in our plans. Let me briefly review what's involved.
   - First, we'll show them that the current way is not the best choice to meet the company's objectives and initiate discussions of a different way currently under consideration that would get better results. That will help demonstrate the need for the change.
   - Then we'll ask those involved in the change, what they find good about the benefits of the new way. Help them see themselves already having and enjoying this new product/service.
   - Next, we'll talk about what will change and what won't change. And we'll challenge them to find the Benefits in each change, especially how each change solves specific problems and removes ill-

effects of not changing (Support, Challenge, and Support).

- We'll want to make sure they know about the support, training, supervision and other resources available to them.

- Then it's time to engage them in developing ways they will implement each change that's required of them. We'll let them decide where they have the expertise and experience. Where they lack the necessary expertise, we'll encourage them to make recommendations.

- Finally, collectively we'll sit down and develop and agree on a clear path and plan to get these changes they now want. Keep in mind that people generally don't resist something they helped to create.

The sequence can change as needed. If that makes sense to you, let's put the change management steps in the overall plan. The bonus is that you can use these principles and steps for other changes you're making in your business."

Response Strategies:

1. "That's not an uncommon challenge. To meet it, we've developed a comprehensive plan of action to help smooth the way and minimize resistance. Let's review the steps to see if this will work with your staff."

2. "Certainly, we're prepared for some resistance and we need to plan how to compensate, neutralize, and offset it. From our experience, we know where resistance will happen and we know how to mitigate it." Now discuss your change management process. Review your strategies to gain input and engagement with those affected by the change. Let them decide where they

have the expertise and experience. Where they lack the expertise, let them make recommendations. Keep in mind that people generally don't resist something they helped create.

84. Objection: *We need time to adjust to this.*

When? After the presentation or demonstration.
Probable Cause: Prospect does not believe the plan will succeed. There are too many unsettling uncertainties. With this objection, they are no longer resisting, instead, they are facing the grief process involving the loss of how they did it before. Or they are through the grief process and are just trying to wrap their minds around how they will implement.
Objective: Develop a detailed plan of action with the prospect's input.

Prevention Strategies:

1. Your plan should include how you will help them deal with the grief process over what they are giving up or losing. The component of the Change Management Process that helps with this is when you tell them what will change and what will not change. The supporting role you can play to help them through the grief process is to use your Active Listening Skills, especially "reflecting emotion." Recognize the feeling of loss they're experiencing. Sometimes naming the emotion works and sometimes a few minutes of silence is all that's needed. Change can be unsettling and upsetting to some people and you should be prepared to use the three-step method to Defuse Anger (Recognize, Apologize, and Solutionize). That will also help pull

them through the sadness phase of the grief process and help move them to objectivity.

2. Engage the prospect in developing the steps as needed to ensure they feel comfortable with each step and each phase of the project. Engage more and more people in the plan at the level where they will be impacted the most.

3. Be goal oriented and continually focus on the positive aspects of the change and in your conversations. Don't mope if they mope. Defuse the emotions, problem-solve with an eye on setting achieving a smooth change. This gives them something to look forward to.

4. Use one or more or a combination of the Step-Based Closing Strategies to reduce anxieties.

Preemption Strategies:

1. This is similar to the previous objection "I'm not comfortable with this yet." But it is also different in the quality of the objection. They may, in fact, be comfortable with what needs to happen, but they need time to adjust to a new reality that those steps will create. As such, your biggest obstacle will be the "grief process" they, by definition, must go through. Help them move through the change process. In brief, use your Active Listening Skills, Defusing Anger, and Change Management strategies to help move them through the process. See the Prevention Strategies above for additional information.

2. Anger is a part of the grief process. So if the change is significant and personal, then be prepared to defuse the emotions using the three-step Defusing Anger process.

   a. Recognize: Call the emotion by name. This takes the power out of the negative emotion. For example,

"It can be unsettling to have to change after doing it one way for so long."

b. Apologize: Show you care. Offer a generic "no-fault" apology. This releases the sadness emotion. For example, "I'm really sorry that you have to go through this." Or "Sad this is happening now and glad we can figure out how to deal with it."

c. Solutionize: Problem-solve to help prevent further loss and to help recover objectivity and acceptance. For example, "So while that's not going to work anymore, what will happen that's going to feel really good is . . ." Whenever you take something away through change, always, always, always follow it with what you can do phrased in a positive manner.

Response Strategies:

1. "This is a new way to look at it, so I can understand the need for time to adjust. One way that helps in this process is to review the plan for implementation so you have a good visual representation of how this will all come about. You'll see clearly what will change and what won't change. That will help you and your company adjust much easier. Let's start by looking at the critical points and the signs that will tell us we're there."

2. "I understand the adjustment process you'll have to go through. And in particular, I know there will be some grieving over the loss of how things used to be. That's a sad part and I'm sorry you and the team will be going through it. What I want to work with you on now are the communications that will be sent to everyone involved. We need to make sure they understand how

much we care about how the change will affect them and to let them know about the support available to help work through the problems that will inevitably come up during the implementation process."

85. Objection: *Don't know how to tell my supplier "no."*

When? After the presentation or demonstration.

Probable Cause: Prospect does not believe the plan will succeed. Could be friends (or a relative) with the current supplier and does not want to hurt their feelings in any way.

Objective: Develop a detailed plan of action with the prospect's input.

Prevention Strategies:

1. Recognize that if a company has been with a single supplier for some time, this may be a spoken or unspoken objection or roadblock. Be prepared to help.
2. Use a detailed, comprehensive checklist of action items that must be done to implement your solution.
3. Include a logical process with examples of how to tell the current supplier of the change. This should include the basic steps of helping the person manage the shift from loss to the present reality, to a plan for the future. Put this in a sample letter for the prospect to model their written communication.
4. Include contingencies on your list to lower the prospect's anxiety.
5. Use a detailed plan of action at the end of the presentation and slightly emphasize the steps to notify the current supplier.

Preemption Strategies:

1. If there has been a long-term relationship with the current supplier, there could be a block to moving forward. The prospect may postpone the inevitable or perhaps gives the current supplier a chance to counter the deficits (missing Advantages and Benefits of your USPs). Once it's clear that you are going to win the sale, move quickly to focus on how to notify the current supplier. Use the prevention strategies regarding offering sample letters or talking points others have used before.

2. Be aware that some suppliers get very angry when they lose a long-standing customer. Anger is a part of grieving over the loss. And you should also be aware that some salespeople have been known to engage in some questionable strategies to try to sabotage the completion of the sale. For example, they may make a tour of all the people they've worked with to let them know they lost the account, cast aspersions about the new supplier, and indirectly try to get their contacts to intervene on their behalf. Be prepared for this by getting the prospect, now a customer, to take you around and introduce you to people you will be working with before the current supplier is notified. This way you have a chance to begin to establish a relationship, point out some great Benefits using the FAB / TEA approach with each person you meet. Now when the competitor's salesperson goes around to do their dastardly deed (consciously or subconsciously), it will appear as "sour grapes" and backfire.

Response Strategies:

1. "I can understand that you've been with your current supplier for some time and it's not the easiest thing to tell them about the change, even when it is in the best interests of the company. So, to help, we've collected some ideas from other customers on how they did it. Here are some sample scripts of the key points of what they said. And here are a couple of sample letters for your review. Please modify as you feel appropriate. If you'd like, why don't we work on this together now and get it out of the way? That way, if you have any questions or concerns we can work through them together." Now move into a position to discuss the points they would like to include and those they want to exclude.

2. "While it may seem vital at the moment to avoid hurting this supplier's feelings, in the long run, your ability to help your company move forward is what's got to dominate your decision, doesn't it? To do otherwise could put the entire operation at risk, and that just doesn't make sense to you or anyone else." What you're doing is to help them get their priorities back in balance and to point out that others might not take lightly to the fact that they stayed with a less desirable supplier at the expense of the company.

Final Thoughts

Thank you for buying this book. What you learn from it will pay you dividends for years to come. And yes, I've created a "sales strategy book" to help sell this book. Why? It works!

- Bob DeGroot

Objection:
When?
Probable Cause:
Objective:

Prevention Strategies:

Preemption Strategies:

Response Strategies:

Objection:
When?
Probable Cause:
Objective:

Prevention Strategies:

Preemption Strategies:

Response Strategies:

Objection:
When?
Probable Cause:
Objective:

Prevention Strategies:

Preemption Strategies:

Response Strategies:

CPSIA information can be obtained
at www.ICGtesting.com
Printed in the USA
LVOW07s1548070617

537271LV00010B/703/P